RELIGION BY RADIO

RELIGION BY RADIO

Its Place in British Broadcasting

MELVILLE DINWIDDIE
C.B.E., D.S.O., M.C., D.D.

FOREWORD BY THE RIGHT HON. LORD REITH
P.C., G.C.V.O., G.B.E., C.B., D.C.L., LL.D.

London
GEORGE ALLEN AND UNWIN LTD
RUSKIN HOUSE   MUSEUM STREET

FIRST PUBLISHED IN 1968

© George Allen and Unwin Ltd 1968

PRINTED IN GREAT BRITAIN
in 11 on 12 pt Pilgrim
AT THE UNIVERSITY PRESS
ABERDEEN

FOREWORD

'I'm writing an account of religion by radio in its first forty years,' Dr Dinwiddie told me; 'I wish you to give me a foreword of six hundred words.' 'Must you call it religion by radio?' I asked; 'Six hundred words,' he replied. So here they are.

Religion by radio – probably relatively the most ineffectual or anyhow the most inefficient – in engineering or commercial sense of effort to result – of all the sectional activities of broadcasting. . . . But better begin at the beginning – Dr Dinwiddie's beginning with broadcasting and the BBC in June 1933.

I was spending a weekend with Sir George and Lady Lilian Adam Smith in Aberdeen; and on the Saturday evening we had been talking about the search for a BBC regional director for Scotland; it had been going on for some time; the need had been giving me a good deal of concern. For any English post, there were plenty of candidates; for a Scottish post – very few or none; much discussion on that Saturday evening about the qualifications and qualities required.

Sunday morning to King's College Chapel; in the evening – had I ever been in St Machar's Cathedral, and would I like to go there? 'No and Yes respectively.' Quite impressed by the minister; they told me afterwards that he had graduated MA in Edinburgh just in time to join up at the outbreak of the 1914 war; he had returned a major with the DSO, Military OBE, MC and Mentions. His last job was a Deputy Assistant Adjutant-General, GHQ in France. He had been persuaded to stay on in the Army for four years – staff captain in the War Office; but he had become increasingly uneasy. Had war not come when it did, he would have proceeded immediately after his MA degree to a BD; then to ordination and the ministry of the Church of Scotland. Despite much blandishment and many attractive

7

offers, he had retired from the Army and gone back to Edinburgh University. He had been minister of St Machar's Cathedral for nearly eight years – 3,500 members, fifty elders. Quite a fellow, I thought; and returned that night to London.

Some time later a letter came from Lady Lilian; did I think the minister I had heard, and heard about, might do for the Scottish directorship? I said I could not answer till I had had not just a good talk with him but a very good talk; did she think he would care to consider, and to be considered for, the post? Lady Lilian definitely thought Yes. 'Shall I ring him and ask him – on the above assumption – to come to London?' 'Yes,' she said; and forthwith I did.

Two days later we were surveying each other – Mr Dinwiddie and I – across a large table in Broadcasting House, London. Explanation by me, in less than a minute but comprehensively as to essentials; question and answer north to south, question and answer south to north; an hour of it but quick moving all the time – and, incidentally, how one longs that people should be compelled to display a number indicating their intelligence quotient, so that one might be warned in advance and know when to speak slowly, proceed carefully from one statement to the next, words of one syllable, and all the rest of it.

In due course Mr Dinwiddie said that the next question was to be his last; a rather personal one, he advised; he hoped I would not object to it. 'Will you yourself be in the BBC for many years yet; can you assure me of that? This is a vital issue to me.' My reply was that, for lots of reasons, I could not positively assure him of any number of years; but, negatively, I could say that I had then no thought of leaving the BBC; I expected to be where I was for some years yet; I asked if that was enough. 'Yes.'

In five years I was out; he in twenty-five; and to his military orders a civil CBE had been added; to his academic

8

ones a DD of Aberdeen. The Scottish Regional Director had definitely directed and controlled; his interest and supervision had been catholic in the all-embracing significance and ubiquitous. He seemed to be as much concerned with jazz music as in that of the hymn book; in a coon show from Saltcoats as in a service from St Giles' Cathedral. And so, I suppose, he should.

The comment above about ineffectualness and inefficiency of broadcast religious activities is not to any extent chargeable to the transmitting end – conception, planning, mounting, execution; nor to the receiving end as such. It did, and does, apply to follow-up – or rather lack of follow-up – of the transmission at the reception end.

The churches – all denominations and confessions – presumably exist to bring men to a knowledge of, and faith in, Christ; 'Come and see' their supreme commission. In business terms they have something to sell; and, as elsewhere, sales can be vastly increased by, and may to a great extent depend on, advertising. Here millions of pounds worth of advertising had been done for them free. But neither the governing bodies nor the individual salesmen of the ethics have even yet realised how accidental and odd it was that, from the very beginning, and against indifference, ridicule, opposition, the Christian religion and the Sabbath were given positions of privilege and protection in the broadcasting service, which – circumstances having been otherwise and as might have been expected – no protest or petition by the churches (on eventual recognition of what was happening) could have secured for them. Nor, consequentially, did they realise – and such realisation would probably now be too late – what was required by way of follow-up and encouragement to those whose interest had been revived. If they had, there might have been a national revival on a scale hitherto unimagined.

J.C.W.R.

CONTENTS

RELIGION BY RADIO

Its Place in British Broadcasting

INTRODUCTION

The most distinctive mark of our humanity is the ability to exchange ideas. Man must communicate to live, and his power to respond to what he hears and sees places him high in the scale of creation. From the dawn of history men have used this power of speech to inform and influence their hearers. Babel was an early attempt to achieve this by shouting from the top of a tower reaching high to heaven. It ended in a confusion of noise, a 'scattering abroad' of sound. Many other attempts were made to broadcast the human voice before the ether came under the control of man.

Communication is a two-way traffic. The speaker requires a listener or his words are lost whether uttered in the merest whisper or in the raucous tones of the demagogue. And the listener must learn to distinguish the true from the false, sincerity from hypocrisy, the real from the sham. The prophet Elijah was one of the first to discover that God speaks to men in a 'still small voice' as well as in the thunderings on Mount Sinai, where Moses received the commandments of the Almighty. Another means of communication was found by King David, the musician and sweet singer of Israel, who gave his people a hymn book, and so enabled them to express their feelings of thankfulness for God's mercy and goodness. He showed that praise could transmit man's inmost thoughts to God.

History has demonstrated that the reaction of the listener

is liable to wide variation. Paul's eloquence on Mars Hill aroused mixed emotions and frayed tempers, and made it very clear that the spoken word could please or annoy, attract or repel. How different on the Mount in Galilee when Jesus preached to the multitude. That was casting abroad speech at its finest and best – the voice that could still the storm, clear the temple, raise the dead, and speak with authority not a set of prohibitions but positive rules for daily living in every age. What a difference it would have made to the whole course of history and the communication of the Gospel had there been a microphone on that mount and a record of His words and voice made available for all time.

Oral tradition and the transcription of scribes are fallible methods of ensuring the permanence of speech. The margin of error was reduced by the invention of printing. The extension of Christ's Kingdom in the world has been vastly helped by the printed word, and the Bible translated into many languages can be read by both Christian and pagan, and by people of every race and colour. The prayer from the days of the apostles that the Word should have free course and be glorified has been amply fulfilled.

But again there was a limitation because only those who could read and understand would benefit. It has been left to this age of scientific achievement to discover a more rapid and effective means of transmitting human speech. The development of radio in its modern form marks the beginning of a new era of communication. The use of the word 'broadcast' brought back an old term into current use. The sower in the parable cast the seed abroad and, down the centuries, that word has described the method of scattering the seed over the whole surface of the field instead of sowing it in drills. In Dr Johnson's dictionary of 1827, broadcast was defined as 'the process of cultivating seed by sowing it with the hand at large or casting it broadly'.

Luke
8:4-8

And now, by the inventive genius and skill of man, space has been spanned at the rate of light; words can penetrate shut windows and closed doors, and come right into our homes. Radio is, however, subject to individual control and need never intrude. It can be shut off when not wanted and yet be available when most likely to be welcomed. It is mass communication without mass effect, because it can be received into the family circle of twos and threes – innumerable small groups shorn of crowd emotion and yet easily moved by sincerity and truth. For good or ill, radio is the most vital contribution of science to this generation. Of course, human nature being what it is, there is always the risk of the listener overhearing what is not meant for him, or hearing something he does not understand nor enjoy, with consequent irritation or criticism. This applies specially to religious items and one of the most real and persistent fears of the clergy and church people in the early days was that such broadcasts might be heard by pagans and unbelievers.

Religion by radio began at a time when the scepticism created by the First World War still exerted a strong influence. Thanksgivings for victory in a war to end war had faded and, though trade and commerce were booming in Britain, a feeling of instability was apparent in society, with a failure to maintain moral standards and rise to new opportunities of service. There was a superficial gaiety in all walks of life, but war had blunted man's sensibility, and a reverence for the welfare of others was lacking in days of hard-won peace. As General Smuts so well expressed it, 'A new heart must be given, not only to our enemies, but also to us; a new spirit of generosity and humanity born in the hearts of people in the great hour of common suffering and sorrow.' It was a time of pause in social change subject to what Sidney Webb called 'the inevitability of gradualness'. It was still a world without H bombs or ballistic missiles, airliners, talkie films or television, penicillin or football pools – before even the beginning of the welfare state.

Thus the stage was set in this needy age to 'cast abroad', like bread upon the waters, the Christian religion by radio, able to reach to the ends of the earth, into the homes of people everywhere – to those of every class, colour and belief, or of none, and so employ this scientific method for the glory of God and the spread of Christ's Kingdom. The marvel of this development through years of poverty and plenty, of unsettled peace and devastating war, of a shrinking world and expanding space, of faith battered and reborn into closer unity, and its influence on the life of a generation – the story of this truly noble enterprise is told in the pages of this book.

CHAPTER I

THE FRAMEWORK OF RELIGIOUS BROADCASTING

Sowing the Seed

'Who hath ears to hear, let him hear'

Beginnings are always exciting. The pioneer in radio is a creative artist whose canvas can span the globe and whose target is the hearing ear and the understanding heart. Policy must determine the pattern of planning, and imaginative ideas supply the content and quality of programmes. It was perhaps natural that a broadcasting company whose General Manager was the son of a Scottish Minister should give high priority to religion as a regular ingredient of its output. Mr Reith wrote that he had been more concerned about the religious policy of the BBC in matters great and small than anything else.

Broadcast Stations were opened in London, Birmingham, and Manchester in November 1922, and new horizons began to appear in music, drama, social and political affairs, with news and information, hitherto available only in print or heard at public meetings, brought directly into the homes of the people. In the religious sphere, broadcasting was immediately confronted with the disunity of Christendom, because the churches had reverted to their denominational isolation after much combined war effort. So sadly were they divided that it would have caused little surprise if religion as such had been entirely omitted from the programmes. The commercial purpose of the Broadcasting Company was to attract purchasers of receivers by providing pleasant home entertainment, and religion might have been regarded as an unnecessary extra. For this and other reasons, the programme planners introduced it very gradually – indeed, for the first year of radio in Britain, only some ten minutes on Sunday evenings were allocated for a religious address. On Christmas Eve, little more than a month after regular daily transmissions began, the address was given by J. A. Mayo, Rector of Whitechapel, who thus had the honour of being the first clergyman to broadcast in Britain. He was followed a week later by Dr Archibald Fleming, Minister of St Columba's (Church of Scotland), who gave a New Year message at midnight on the last night of the old year. So from the very start, barriers of denomination were of less consequence to the BBC than ability to speak at the microphone. The list of preachers who gave the addresses on Sunday evenings during 1923 included a broad mixture – Gipsy Smith, the evangelist, who spoke from the Albert Hall at the first religious outside broadcast; Tubby Clayton, Founder Padre of Toc H; Prebendary Carlile of the Church Army; Father H. Vaughan of the Roman Church; Dr F. W. Norwood of the City Temple; Studdert Kennedy, 'Woodbine Willie' of the 1914-18 war; and Dr Pereira, Bishop of Croydon – truly, a varied assortment.

As time went on, requests were received for a full service to be broadcast, but doubts were expressed as to whether it would be suitable for radio. Mr Reith went to Archbishop Randall Davidson for help and advice; he was invited to listen to an address transmitted by radio, and was so much interested that he agreed to call together representatives of the Churches in England to confer about religious broadcasting. This group formed the first Advisory Committee, known as the 'Sunday Committee'. It met in May 1923 under the chairmanship of Dr Cyril Garbett, then Bishop of Southwark, and discovered a wide area of agreement for the working of this new medium of communication. But many problems had to be solved before a church service could be broadcast. What form of worship; what emphasis on teaching; what aim and purpose in preaching should be pursued? Then a choice had to be made between the varied methods of conducting religious services, the different versions of the Bible, the many hymn books in use and the diversity of church praise before a definite policy could be worked out. In December 1923, Mr Reith, now Managing Director of the Company, wrote in *Radio Times*, which had begun publication that autumn, 'It has been decided to try another experiment. We are going to broadcast a complete church service – without prejudice to any denomination. If the result is satisfactory, we shall be guided by our representative Sunday Committee in the matter of further broadcasts of a similar character.' On January 6, 1924, a service was relayed from St Martin-in-the-Fields. Dick Sheppard was willing to undertake the experiment, but was doubtful whether the music of his church would be suitable for radio transmission. He also anticipated some criticism, and asked that the Sunday Committee should send a formal letter of invitation to his church council so that he might assure them that he was not 'trying to fix up any sort of stunt with the Broadcasting Company'. He wanted to make it clear that the request for facilities came from a body representing more than one denomination. This service brought so many letters of appreciation that a series of broadcasts was arranged for the second Sunday of each month at 8 o'clock. The preachers were to include men from other denominations in addition to the Church of England, thus beginning a united witness in Britain. Dick Sheppard described these monthly relays as an endeavour to provide 'a simple service for all', a proclamation of the Gospel to him that hath ears to hear. This was literally true, because crystal sets and earphones were in general use at that time, and it was said that eighty per cent of the population within crystal range would get an earful of religion by radio.

Local stations, of which there were more than twenty at that time, some with their own advisory bodies, were under no obligation to take the St Martin's service. As there was only one programme, most of them preferred to relay acts of worship from churches in their own areas, probably a wise practice in view of the wide differences of form and practice. It was not until the Daventry high-power station opened in 1925, when the national network covered the whole of England, that the monthly service from St Martin's became available as an alternative choice. Scotland and Wales were in due course included, and it is interesting to reflect on the reaction of listeners of very different religious practice to Anglican services heard by radio. Criticism was to some extent avoided by prominent preachers from all over Britain being invited to take part in these broadcasts. Many clergymen were also critical of listening to worship on earphones. Even the highest ecclesiastical authorities were suspicious and had to be convinced that complete acts of worship could be broadcast without blasphemy. The Armistice Day service of 1923 and the relay of the wedding of a member of the Royal Family from Westminster Abbey were refused. The reasons given were that 'the services would be received by a considerable number of persons in an irreverent manner, and might even be heard by persons in public houses with their hats on'. It was not until some years later that the Dean and Chapter of St Paul's Cathedral gave permission for broadcasts from that great building though other churches in the metropolis were ready to provide facilities.

Antagonism from atheists and agnostics was to be expected. A letter published in *Radio Times* in the autumn of 1923 evoked the reply from a freethinker that such items as religious services were futile and unnecessary and should be stopped. In the correspondence which followed, the concensus of opinion was so definitely in favour of their continuance that the advice of the Sunday Committee to extend them became the policy of the BBC. Religious items increased and were to be found in the programmes on weekdays as well as on Sundays. Special broadcasts for children were included, and Evensong was relayed from Westminster Abbey on Thursday afternoons from October 1926. About the same time, the epilogue was introduced as the closing item on Sundays. Mr Reith had asked that the programme that evening should end on a religious note, but it had been difficult to insert such an item at the close of a popular concert. It was decided to have a separate item consisting of a hymn, a few verses of scripture, and a psalm. There was no prayer out of deference for those who were unaccustomed to saying or hearing prayers, though such well-known hymns as 'Abide With Me' and 'Nearer my God to Thee', were greatly appreciated. The London Station Director, B. E. Nicolls, suggested the title Epilogue, and so this most appropriate way of ending Sunday listening was started and had become one of the permanent features of broadcasting. A listener described it as 'a perfect benediction'.

In December 1926, Hugh Johnston, Vicar of Cranleigh and a former curate of St Martin's, was asked to take a daily service as an experiment. Many requests for such an item had been received from listeners, especially invalids and old folk – indeed, a petition had been signed by thousands of people for a half-hour service every day in the afternoon. Although there were as yet no regular morning transmissions, it was decided that a fifteen-minute service at ten-fifteen each weekday morning would be most suitable. The experiment was so well received and appreciated by patients in hospital and the housebound, that the BBC was inundated with some 8,000 letters suggesting subjects for prayer to meet personal needs. Even busy housewives made time to listen, and so began an item which was to continue in peace and war, in times of joy and sorrow, and which still attracts a large and appreciative audience.

It is difficult now to realise the limitations of the programme schedules in these early days. Broadcasting normally began at five o'clock on Sunday afternoons and on week-days, apart from the daily service and a few morning items, transmissions did not start until late afternoon. Technical research, however, quickly extended listening facilities. The high-power station at Daventry, using a wavelength of 1500 metres, gave improved transmission and clearer reception. The increasing use of loudspeakers (the large horn type was then a novelty and sold for the modest sum of around thirty-five shillings in the mid-twenties), made earphones unnecessary, and altered the whole character of home listening. In the religious sphere, it meant that church services and other items would be heard in groups rather than in isolation with the family as the normal unit.

Experiment and research also helped the development of simultaneous broadcasts – known techically as SB – a system which had been used mainly for news and special items. The autonomy of local stations, so much a feature of the early years, resulting from shortage of staff and equipment, was being curtailed by the rapid advance of scientific progress. For religious items, technical changes brought new problems. How far should Sunday services be shared? And how could the needs of local churches be conserved with increased centralisation? If the purpose of this new medium of communication was to make people better Christians, could this be achieved more effectively by local or national broadcasts? Entertainment programmes in the twenties had found their main support in local talent, and it was argued that the same policy should be applied to religion. But there was a vital difference in dealing with the Gospel of Christ, the ultimate unity of which demanded the sharing of resources, and a search for more common ground between denominations, if this unity was to be more than an ideal.

For the first ten years of broadcasting in Britain there was no special staff for the planning and presentation of religious items. In London, J. C. Stobart, an educationist on the programme staff, was asked to look after religion in addition to his own work. He became deeply absorbed in it, and gave much thought to the policy and preparation of services and other items. When he died in 1933, his fine contribution to the development of religious broadcasting received many well-deserved tributes.

At local stations, any member of staff who had time to spare was given the task of supervising religious items. It was little wonder that they suffered from lack of planning and co-ordination until there was a full-time Director of Religion. F. A. Iremonger, Editor of *The Guardian*, a Church of England weekly, was appointed and took up his duties in July 1933. He brought system and a definite policy into this most important sphere of broadcasting, and welded into a team those in charge of religion in London and the regions. He acted as Secretary to the Central Religious Advisory Committee, known as CRAC, and was able to exert a guiding influence on the deliberations of regional committees. His genial personality and constructive attitude to the wider aspects of radio made him also a consultant and adviser on questions of moral standards, especially in connection with Sunday items, a vitally important function in helping to ensure that only the best was broadcast, and that there was nothing to offend. He became a 'father-in-God' to many members of staff, and exercised a unique ministry in its breadth and usefulness. But perhaps the greatest contribution to radio of Freddie Iremonger, as he was familiarly called, was the preparation of the Coronation broadcast of 1937, and his remarkable and deeply reverent commentary of that great event. He retired from the BBC in 1939 and became Dean of Lichfield. His splendid work was recognised by a well-merited doctorate from Glasgow University.

The thirties had begun with the economy of the country at a low ebb and with many unemployed, following the sudden and complete collapse of post-war prosperity in America. Poverty was widespread in Britain; cynics were active against Church and State, and religious faith was far from easy when the essential need of so many people was to secure the bare necessities of life. The churches rose to the challenge of the emergency, and showed a fine spirit of service in bringing the comforts of life and the encouragement of religion to the needy and despairing. Clubs were organised for those without work and kitchens provided soup for the hungry. Broadcasting was used to make known the deep concern of church people for those in need without distinction of class or creed, and showed radio as a useful ally of organised religion.

In spite of the poverty of that period, receiving licences continued to increase. The amount of programme time devoted to religion also increased, and an estimate of the number of religious items broadcast over the whole of Britain in 1932 was ample evidence of steady expansion. From a mere fifteen minutes in 1922, nearly four hours each week were given to religion ten years later, and some ten million licence-holders and their households could hear them. Many choices were also available for those who took the trouble to tune into a particular station, though there was no secular alternative to religious services. The most any listener could do was a bit of sermon-tasting, if he was willing to exercise tolerance and gain understanding by hearing the worship of different denominations. The range of choice was passing to those at the receiving end. Full details of services and other religious items were published in *Radio Times* and the press, and *The Listener*, which began publication in 1929, printed excerpts from broadcast sermons. Those who based their religious life on radio were able to become sincere 'receivers of the Word'. Regular items gradually built up their own audience of those ready to keep tryst with their loudspeakers alone or in family groups. The initial opposition of the churches had not only died down, but had turned into an eagerness to use this medium for the proclamation of the Gospel.

Many developments took place in the years before the Second World War. The Empire Service of the BBC began officially in 1932, and opened up vast possibilities of establishing and maintaining contact with Christians all over the world, and making the Gospel available to those of every race and religion who were able to listen.

Another major contribution was made by two series of addresses, 'God and the World through Christian Eyes' and 'The Way to God'. They dealt with fundamental beliefs, and presented the faith in a comprehensive manner. The speakers were chosen for their intellectual ability rather than their denominational affiliation. It was hoped that listeners would be urged to think more about their personal religion, and that the addresses would result in discussion by groups and argument in the family circle. Pamphlets were issued and correspondence was stimulated. But listeners were reluctant to study the basic truths of religion by radio. The series made little impact outside the membership of the churches.

Considerable audience reaction was voiced, however, in 1936 when the Corporation decided to revise the Sunday programme schedules and permit alternatives to religious items. A service was already broadcast at nine-thirty that morning, and had been accepted by clergy and church authorities with considerable misgivings. It was also decided to begin transmissions of secular items after that service on Sundays instead of the late afternoon. The BBC had to receive much listener criticism and meet deputations from the Lord's Day Observance Society as well as from others who were trying, often with difficulty, to maintain the sanctity of the Sabbath. Such protests are now of little more than academic interest, but they are useful reminders of the concern of church people at that time to express their fear of a Continental Sunday being introduced into Britain.

War brought drastic reductions in broadcasting. Only one composite programme for the whole country was permitted for reasons of security until February 1940 when a second, known at first as the Forces Programme, was brought into operation. The religion department in London was moved to Bristol and later to Bedford, making its organisation much more difficult. This was in many ways a return to the very early days of the twenties with only a single programme.

The Daily Service and the Sunday Epilogue never ceased to be broadcast, but listeners everywhere had to hear the same Sunday services or none – a demonstration of unity in an emergency dictated by technical restrictions. More religious items were gradually included both on Sundays and week-days and, when the crisis deepened, short acts of intercession were broadcast each night after the nine o'clock news, and often at the close of the evening's programmes. As was to be expected, war with its national and personal tensions aroused greater interest in religion and gave radio a unique opportunity to meet this need.

In 1940, religious programmes began to assume a certain stability and a recognised shape in the struggle against a ruthless and pagan enemy. Outside broadcasts from churches were resumed, though their locality could not be given, and regional items were allowed on the wavelengths allotted to them. Dr James Welch had succeeded Freddie Iremonger as Director of Religious Broadcasting, and an adequate staff was appointed to serve under him. Eric Fenn, a minister of the English Presbyterian Church; Cyril Taylor, a talented musician; John Williams, and A. C. F. Beales, made an able team in the war years.

One of the first innovations in wartime was an early morning item, a kind of spiritual exercise, coupled with a series of physical jerks, at seven-thirty on weekdays. It began in Scotland in December 1939, with the title 'Lift up your hearts; a thought for the day', and it served to remind listeners of the constant need for God's power and love in the dark days of war. It was heard by a large audience, and survived the war as a regular morning item, though the Daily Dozen stopped soon after the end of hostilities. After twenty-five years in its original form, the title was changed and the content varied to attract a wider audience.

The Forces Programme was provided for members of the Armed Services on land, sea, and in the air, and also became popular with relatives at home, war workers, and those who wanted easy background listening, because it included much light music. Religion found a place in that programme, and this resulted in another innovation – the creation of a radio personality who could speak to and gain the confidence of those on military service. Ronald Selby Wright of the Canongate Kirk in Edinburgh, himself a Chaplain with Army Service both at home and overseas, was chosen for this important work. He became known as the Radio Padre and, in his friendly manner and simple straightforward way of talking at the microphone, broadcast to a remarkable audience of serving personnel, their families, and friends. His influence was wide and far-reaching, and of great value in bringing the essence of the Gospel to those who longed for comfort and encouragement in anxious days, and to others who felt the need of a working faith in such trying times. His talks continued to be heard for some years after the war on both national and regional wavelengths.

Another religious item for easy listening found its way into the Forces Programme. The Sunday Half-hour of Community Hymn Singing was intended for all who could enjoy and perhaps benefit by singing together, whatever their attitude might be to worship and organised religion. Besides reviving the habit of hymn-singing, it became a very popular introduction to the simple truths of Christianity, and still continues as a regular item in what has become the Light Programme.

The most significant development of the war years was, however, the presentation of a cycle of twelve plays by Dorothy L. Sayers, *The Man born to be King*. The voice of Jesus had to be impersonated and, though there was considerable opposition in some quarters, members of the advisory committee in London, representing different denominations, gave their support to the project. The play cycle was first broadcast in 1942 when the war was at its most critical stage, and has been repeated many times on the 'Sound' programmes with almost universal acceptance. The impact of this series will be examined in more detail in a later chapter.

Towards the end of hostilities, a change became apparent in the aim and purpose of religious broadcasting, and a more positive and vigorous proclamation of the Gospel was noticeable. Services of worship were altered in form and content to meet the limitations of the microphone, and new methods of presentation were adopted in the post-war years. More emphasis was placed on evangelism and it was found that the united witness of the churches, so much a feature of these tragic years of conflict, made a more profound impression on the listening public.

In the meantime, the position of the church in the life of the country had been under serious consideration. A report, *Towards the Conversion of England*, had been prepared for the Anglican Convocation, and another *God's Will in our Time* for the General Assembly of the Church of Scotland. Their aim was to assess the most urgent needs of the nation after so much suffering and sorrow. Emphasis was laid on the positive, practical implications of the Christian message of salvation, and in what ways the very large audience to sound broadcasting, still unaffected by television (which had been shut down during the war), could be brought into the orbit of organised religion in the churches, or at least, be influenced in their daily lives by Christian standards.

One of the most insistent post-war requests was that the Service of Holy Communion should be broadcast. This raised many problems – ecclesiastical, technical, and social. It would be an entirely new departure from the recognised practice of some twenty-five years of broadcasting in Britain. It might also be at variance with the traditions of the churches, whose central rite and most cherished Sacrament might be cheapened and discredited if overheard by unbelievers in wrong surroundings and unsuitable conditions. These problems will be discussed in the chapter on worship, but the general policy had to be decided, and it proved to be the most difficult and fundamental ever taken by the religion department of the BBC on the recommendation of their advisory committees. In 1947 this service was offered to listeners as an experiment. The result was a deep and moving appreciation from a large audience, mostly of sick and invalid people, who regarded it as a privilege to participate in their own homes or in hospital. Out of the crucible of tragedy and war had come a new and successful method of bringing the very heart of the Gospel of Jesus Christ to those who wanted to share in its benefits in days of peace.

The Report of the Broadcasting Committee under the Chairmanship of Lord Beveridge, published in 1949, restated the policy of the BBC in the religious field as 'a positive attitude towards Christian values, to safeguard them and foster acceptance of them'. The application of this policy over the years culminated in a most impressive number and variety of items, not only on Sundays, but spread over every day of the week – services, talks, discussions, dramatic presentations of religious themes for schools, children at home, youth, and indeed for all who cared to listen. The staff of the religion department, both in London and the regions, had grown to meet the increasing demands of listeners and viewers. Francis House succeeded Dr James Welch in 1947, and was assisted by clergymen of different traditions, seconded as in the case of Agnellus Andrew from the Roman Church, or appointed to carry out their calling in this new and important sphere. Canon Roy McKay became Head of Religious Broadcasting in 1955 and additional staff, including a lady, Elsie Chamberlain, a minister of the Congregational Church, were required to cope with television, which was restarted in 1946 and added to the responsibility of the department to discover how best to use another powerful method of communicating religious truth. In his book *Take Care of the Sense*, Roy McKay deals with many of the problems involved in bringing the Christian religion convincingly to viewers.

From such beginnings and background, the message of the love of God to man was 'cast abroad', and brought a new dimension into the religious life of the British people. In the entrance hall of Broadcasting House, London, are inscribed the Latin words – *Deus incrementus dat* – God gives the increase. This truly describes the amazing expansion of religious broadcasting.

CHAPTER II

ADVICE FROM THE CHURCHES

The Seed and the Soil

'All things to all men'

When in doubt, set up a committee – this familiar action in a democratic society was the first step taken to give guidance to religious broadcasting. The formation of an advisory body in 1923 has already been noted. The sequence of events that led up to it has been dramatically described in the biography of Archbishop Randall Davidson by Bishop Bell, and by Professor Asa Briggs in *The Birth of Broadcasting*. They tell how Mr Reith went to see the Archbishop on March 16th, some four months after the start of radio as a public service. They dined together on the 20th, when he and his wife heard a programme for the first time. They were 'entirely amazed' at what they heard and the Archbishop expressed himself as 'very much interested in the possibilities of wireless'. The following day he invited a group of representative churchmen to meet on April 20th 'to discuss the use which could rightly and profitably be made of broadcasting on Sundays and especially on Sunday evenings. Ought there to be a religious element? If so, what? And by whom arranged? The officers of the broadcasting company, whose aim is obviously a high one, are anxious to have wise advice.' The meeting took place in the Archbishop's room in the House of Lords. Bishop Garbett, Canon C. S. Woodward and Dick Sheppard represented the Church of England; Dr R. C. Gillie spoke for the Presbyterians, while Thomas Nightingale, a Methodist, was the representative of the Free Churches, and Herbert Ward kept a watching brief for the Roman Catholics. The group welcomed the two principles suggested by the General Manager, that there should be no broadcasts during the hours of public worship, and that there should be a religious item every Sunday evening. Bishop Garbett was nominated chairman of a committee of fourteen which held its first meeting on May 18th, 1923. Thus began the means of obtaining advice for the best use of this new medium.

The committee had to frame a policy with the help of the staff of the company. Mr Reith showed such interest that he took charge of its work, though he encouraged the chairman to help as much as possible. Bishop Garbett, however, adhered strictly to the role of adviser and was always available for consultation, but preferred not to take the initiative, especially where other denominations than his own were involved.

Advisory committees are in a peculiar position in relation to the bodies they are set up to advise. They may be formed casually without much consideration of their terms of reference and membership; they may be used as a safety valve to allow troublesome people to let off steam in offering advice that may not be accepted, or they may become merely a defence mechanism against public criticism. The BBC was concerned with so many facets of social life that it was only too ready to get guidance on matters of special difficulty. The religious committees, both in London and at local stations, found in practice that their advice was gladly received. This was often the result of good chairmanship, and Bishop Garbett proved himself a first-rate chairman, with a capacity for keeping peace without compromise. As his biographer, Charles

Smyth, expressed it, 'With modesty of demeanour, he combined great natural dignity; people did not want to argue with him. He never attempted to load the dice in favour of the Church of England, or showed any partiality for broadcasters of his own persuasion. There was no place in his mind for the denominational spirit in broadcasting.' The wide area of agreement reached under his wise leadership was quite remarkable. Local committees were also well served by able chairmen, though they were subjected to many pressures. They were at first reluctant to co-operate fully with the central body, and at times seemed to assume executive powers in the selection of preachers and churches from which relays should take place. It became evident that the quality of their advice varied a good deal. In some of the smaller stations, every clergyman expected almost as a right to be given a turn at the microphone. When technical progress made it possible to ensure wider coverage from fewer transmitters, the central committee recommended that, in addition to the regular relays from St Martin's on the second Sunday of the month, another service without secular alternative should be available from a church selected from lists submitted by local committees. Closer co-operation resulted and, when the original low-power transmitters were replaced by others with higher power and wider coverage, the country was able to be divided into regions, six in number, though London was for a time also one for administrative purposes. This enabled regional committees to be set up in place of the local bodies that had done so much in the pioneering days. To ensure a co-ordinated policy, the chairmen of the newly formed committees became *ex-officio* members of CRAC and so made a direct contribution to the national development of religious broadcasting.

Before long, however, the membership of these re-organised bodies raised problems for the BBC. From the somewhat casual choice of those who should represent

the diverse elements of the Church, to be selected as a
member of such a committee became a coveted honour
The number from each denomination was questioned, and
the Corporation was asked to relate the membership of
CRAC to the strength of the different churches. Those that
were national and established claimed more members, and
some of the smaller sects urged that their influence as well
as their numbers should be the criterion for representation
The BBC agreed to maintain a loose but reasonable balance
and wisely reserved to itself the responsibility of inviting
members to serve, not as elected or nominated representa
tives of their denomination, but as individuals in their own
right. This in turn led to a certain amount of critical com
ment from those who wanted to nominate their own
representatives. There was an obvious need for consulta
tion before invitations were issued, and this practice was
adopted with satisfactory results. Early suspicion of radio
as a method of propagating the faith had been replaced by
competition to give advice and to get an adequate share
of broadcasts. As the years passed, there emerged a source
of good objective advice from men of wide experience
For a time the members of these committees laid upon
themselves a self-denying ordinance not to broadcast
except on special occasions to avoid any risk of partiality
or privileged access to the microphone. Membership re
mained static for seventeen years except for vacancies
caused by death or resignation. It was not until after the
war that a scheme of rotation was adopted.

One of the main tasks of CRAC when it was first set up
was to recommend speakers for the ten-minute address on
Sunday evenings. The decision in 1923 to broadcast a
complete church service enlarged its functions, and en
tailed a selection of churches from which relays should
take place with advice on the choice of clergymen to
broadcast from church or studio. As often happens at the
start of any new venture, people personally known to

those responsible were chosen, and preference was naturally given to men who showed an interest in this medium,
so long as they were otherwise suitable. We have seen
that St Martin-in-the-Fields became the first regular radio
church, and that the addresses at services there were
shared by a small group of preachers. This, however, could
not for long satisfy the rapidly growing audience. The
wide terms of reference of CRAC were to provide 'all
things to all men' – to attempt the impossible task of
meeting the religious need of thousands of listeners of
many different types and tastes and, at the same time, deal
with requests and sometimes demands for broadcasts from
churches and smaller sects that wanted to give expression
to their particular beliefs. Was St Martin's the only church
to qualify for regular relays? And was the choice of men
invited to give the addresses wide enough to include the
best preachers in Britain? Scotland with its national church
was the first to find another radio pulpit in St Cuthbert's,
Edinburgh, which came to be used for monthly services
with preachers of every denomination except Roman
Catholic. By happy coincidence this arrangement began
in 1929, the year of the Union of the old Established and
the United Free churches, and continued for some ten years.

CRAC and the BBC agreed that preaching ability at the
microphone should be the determining factor in those
invited to broadcast but every effort was made to preserve
a balance between the denominations, so that the most
suitable men could be secured without a selection based
strictly on the strength and prestige of the different
churches. In this difficult task, a great responsibility rested
on the members of the central and regional committees in
their efforts to discover the real potential of those who
applied personally – and many did – or those who were
recommended by friends and admirers. Religious broadcasting was in danger of becoming immersed in sectarian
issues.

Every change in traditional practice, especially in religion, is subject to criticism, and considerable opposition continued to come from within the churches. This stemmed from suspicion of anything new and the likely effect on church attendance and public worship, from fears of denominational bias, from jealousies of individuals and groups – prevalent even among Christian people – and from the wide variation of form and practice in worship. To obviate this, the committee reaffirmed the original policy of the Corporation to exclude propaganda or any attempt to proselytise in broadcasts.

The condition requiring a manuscript of the address or sermon to be submitted in advance to the BBC raised some interesting points. From the Presbyterian angle, if a sermon had to be prepared and written out in full before delivery, the habit of extempore preaching would be lost – indeed, reliance on the Holy Spirit to give the preacher his message was called in question, and some men famed for their eloquence in the pulpit refused to broadcast under such conditions. This matter came into prominence for another reason in 1928 when a priest of the Roman Church refused to allow any alterations to be made to his script, which contained a direct historical attack on the Reformation. The Archbishop of Liverpool suggested censorship of the address by a tribunal or an assessor of his denomination. CRAC considered the arguments on both sides, and recommended that scripts must continue to be submitted in advance, at least for studio services, so that contentious matter could be modified or deleted. The BBC retained final editorial responsibility to ensure that nothing was broadcast likely to offend or provoke criticism from the listening audience – a wise and sensible criterion. It was, however, laid down that, in the process of censorship, an appropriate member of CRAC must be consulted in cases of doubt or deletion, and his decision made known to the author of the script. This concession to the Roman Catholic members of the committees avoided friction and smoothed out a difficulty peculiar to radio.

In 1930, the Houses of Convocation received a report by a special committee set up to enquire into 'the religious value of broadcast services, and their bearing on public worship'. Both Houses passed a resolution of grateful appreciation of the service rendered to the cause of religion by the BBC. The Lower House, endorsing the past policy of the Corporation, defined the scope of its activities in this sphere in these broad terms: 'The BBC would claim that its obvious possibilities (bringing religion to the hearth side as a source of comfort to the sick, the isolated, the timid among religious people, and in making the voice of religion, the beauty of worship, and the attractions of scripture known to vast numbers of irreligious or semi-religious outsiders), have been explored and exploited to the utmost with results little short of marvellous; but at the same time, the fact cannot be denied that people whose only religious contact is through listening miss much of the essential influences of religion, and the constant hope of the Corporation is that, as in the field of education, broadcasting may act as a stimulus and as a means of recruitment for the churches.' The report was a landmark in the history of religious broadcasting; the policy of the BBC and CRAC had been vindicated and, after eight years of experiment and expansion, had received official approval.

As has been noted, the general opposition of the churches had turned into appreciation, and though most church members were willing to accept worship in their homes, pressure and criticism from those outside the churches was increasing. Rationalists and freethinkers wanted to be allowed to state their views and argue the merits and demerits of Christianity at the microphone. These requests were refused because such arguments would offend many professing Christians in the listening audience, but the pressure was so vocal and persistent that the BBC had to reaffirm its policy in religion of 'giving offence to no one' and continued to make provision only for non-controversial items in its programme schedules.

It was perhaps natural that sceptics, who had little interest in religion except to criticise it, should demand consideration, but CRAC had to deal with more difficult and delicate requests from sects on the fringe of organised religion. Such bodies as Christian Scientists, Spiritualists, and Unitarians asked to be allotted time on the air. From the start, the committee had recommended that broadcast services should be offered only to churches and denominations in the main stream of the Christian tradition. This became the established policy of the Corporation and, in consequence, those who could be regarded as representing orthodox Christianity were invited to conduct worship, preach, or give talks on religious subjects though, in certain circumstances, others might be allowed time to explain their viewpoint.

Christian Scientists were the first to seek recognition. As early as 1923, CRAC gave serious consideration to their desire to be classed as a Christian denomination, but refused the request and took the view that Christian Science was more a system of faith healing than a church. As Professor Archibald Main of Glasgow, the Scottish member of the central committee, remarked after a long discussion in CRAC, 'They are perhaps not in the main stream, but they have a very big eddy.' It was a difficult decision to reach, because of the name, and the object of their effort – to cure all disease – a truly Christian aim, in line with the healing work of Christ. Although they did not get permission for broadcast services, the possibility was examined of including the tenets of the sect as a controversial topic in a balanced discussion or series of talks, but they were unwilling to allow their beliefs to be presented at the microphone except as a religion. In spite of these efforts to place them in a suitable context, they continued in their demands to participate in religious broadcasts or at least to exert an influence on the policy of the committee. They were helped by having eminent people to support them – the Marquis of Lothian, Lord and Lady Astor, the Earl of Airlie, and others who in the war years especially tried to have the ban lifted, but the Governors of the BBC held to their decision.

Spiritualists were in a somewhat different category. Their principal protagonist was Sir Oliver Lodge, himself a superb broadcaster on scientific subjects. He was one of the speakers in a Sunday afternoon series in 1933 on 'The Future Life', along with J. B. S. Haldane, a sceptic, and Professor Kemp Smith, a positive theist. Sir Oliver spoke in that series as a Spiritualist and explained the nature of his belief in the after-life of the Spirit. It thus resulted in the Spiritualists having their theories explained at the microphone in their appropriate context, though they were not granted facilities for broadcast services or talks. The situation became much more delicate in wartime when they asked to be allowed to give listeners comfort and hope which they regarded as being available in spirit communication with loved ones who had been killed. They claimed that their information on life and survival after death, and on the nature of that survival, was received from the dead themselves – from 'controls' who transmitted the messages through a medium in a trance. There was perhaps a certain affinity to radio with its human speech travelling mysteriously through space, but that ended the similarity. They were not allowed broadcast services.

The attitude of the Unitarians and their insistent demands raised yet another type of problem. This stemmed from the worship of the sect in Britain compared with the United States. In the early twenties, some Unitarian services had been broadcast from local stations, but in

1931 CRAC recommended that no preacher should broadcast if he belonged to a denomination that did not recognise the divinity of Christ. This theological test was difficult to apply, but it definitely excluded Unitarians. The BBC was not fully convinced, however, that all Unitarian preachers should be kept from the microphone, and a sharp difference of opinion became apparent between the advisory committee and those it was appointed to advise. A solution was eventually found under which the BBC accepted full responsibility for inviting prominent Unitarians to preach, provided they did not use the occasion to proselytise. The door was thus left open and some eleven broadcasts took place over a period of five years. No representation of Unitarian bodies was allowed on CRAC, but their preachers had a contribution to make in assessing the place of religion in a humanist age, and it seemed reasonable that they should be heard.

Many other sects asked to be given opportunities to broadcast. Some such as Jehovah's Witnesses, Seventh Day Adventists, and Christadelphians, were refused, while the Salvation Army, the Society of Friends, the Brotherhood Movement, and the Evangelical Alliance, were occasionally heard. A difficult border-line case was the Oxford Group, later known as Moral Rearmament, which made many demands that they should be allowed to describe their aims and methods. Dr Frank Buchman, a Minister of the Lutheran Church in America, paid frequent visits to this country as founder of the Group, which specialised in house parties and meetings where members recounted their experiences of God's guidance in their personal lives. Dr Buchman gathered round him people of every walk of life and his methods of modern publicity and persuasion were novel and effective. But he asserted that religion was not essentially a matter of intellect or of the heart, but of the will. It was a system, a way of life rather than a creed, and the worship of the Group was quite unorthodox. It eventually found its radio presentation in a series in 1938 entitled 'The Validity of Religious Experience' in which Dr Buchman took part.

The Ethical Union used yet another line of approach to the BBC. Its members wanted to uphold the independence of ethics as the fundamental and universal principle of personal and social behaviour. They asked to be allowed to conduct their teaching at the microphone, not in competition with any religious faith, but to further their purpose of moral regeneration. They could hardly be regarded as a church or sect, and it was left to the Talks Department of the Corporation to deal with their request. The assistance of CRAC in sorting out the relative position of these bodies in the years of rapid development up to the outbreak of war was of very real value to the BBC, and showed the erudition and wisdom of the members and their broad objective judgement.

War brought its own problems. Perhaps the most troublesome was whether clergymen with pronounced pacifist outlook should be permitted to broadcast. After a sermon by Leyton Richards in 1940, the question was considered by CRAC and, for once, it was found that the members were unable to recommend an agreed policy. The Governors of the BBC took up the matter because of its seriousness, and issued a statement which made it clear that complete freedom of speech could not be allowed in the emergency of war, and that this restriction applied to clergymen equally with other speakers. Every aspect of broadcasting, including religion, must be in sympathy with the nation's struggle for survival, and it was suggested that prayers for victory should be included regularly in broadcasts because of the righteous cause for which we were fighting. For these reasons, it would have been inconsistent to invite any known member of an organisation or any individual who did not hold these views to speak at the microphone. In consequence, such preachers as

Donald Soper of Tower Hill fame, George MacLeod of the
Iona Community, and Charles Raven, a Cambridge Don –
all experienced and popular radio personalities – were
debarred from broadcasting. Some prominent churchmen,
including Archbishop Temple, then at York, and Nathaniel
Micklem, of Mansfield College, Oxford, questioned the
wisdom of this veto, but the Governors refused to modify
their ruling and it remained in force until the matter
assumed a much wider significance. The position was discussed in the House of Commons and, as a result, statements were made by the Prime Minister and the Minister
of Information which somewhat modified the previous
policy. The formula finally agreed was in these terms:
'Although it is not the custom of the BBC to invite to the
microphone in war time certain individuals who are known
to be opposed to the national effort, and whose influence
– which would be increased by broadcasting – is used
against that effort, clergymen who sincerely hold pacifist
views are not excluded from the work of religious broadcasting. Pacifist views, however, may not be broadcast.'
This very real and difficult issue of the war period is seen
in a different light from the vantage point of the inter-
vening years, and it is evident that a much greater sense
of freedom has gradually come into broadcast presentation. The door of controversy has been opened wider and
wider since the war in every sphere of radio as well as in
religion. Every aspect of the Christian faith has come on
to the anvil of hard argument and discussion, not only on
Sunday but in such week-end items as 'Any Questions',
and the television 'Brains Trust' when the panel of speakers has included clergymen and bishops ready to give their
views on both secular and religious questions. The result
has been that many issues of immediate and theological
interest have been ventilated, and listeners and viewers
have been given knowledge in a way they could understand to enable them to form their own judgement.

CHAPTER III

WORSHIP AT HOME

Receiving the Word with Joy

'In Spirit and in Truth'

Worship is a fundamental human instinct. It has almost infinite variety of practice, and is of such subjective personal quality that it can vary even in families and among friends. The person or object of most worth is worshipped with an intensity and devotion in proportion to the awe and reverence, the affection and loyalty engendered. This is perhaps a simplification of a very complex habit, but it will serve our purpose. Imagination plays an important part in worship and, though it is easier to express the worth that is felt for someone present and visible or for an object that can be touched and handled, it is possible also to offer that worship to an unseen God when approached in suitable surroundings. Down the centuries, buildings dedicated to Christian worship have been recognised as places where people come together to offer their united worship to God, and these buildings have been consecrated as churches for this purpose. When, however, home is substituted for church, and the congregation is replaced by individuals or members of a family, a very different situation arises. The discipline of gathering in a sacred building no longer applies; there is freedom to move or remain seated, to hear or merely overhear, to concentrate or allow the attention to wander, to take part in the praise, prayers, and readings, or accept passively what is being enacted in distant church or studio.

The first religious broadcasts were most appreciated by the sick, invalid, and aged listeners and, in the era of ear phones, it was very much as isolated individuals that they tuned in to their crystal sets. When loudspeakers came into general use, it was more difficult to shut out extrane ous noises, both human and technical, and adjustments were required to make worship real at home. Sitting in ar armchair by the fire instead of on a hard-backed pew ir church could be a relief but was also a handicap, and the tendency to drop off to sleep during the sermon, not un known even in uncomfortable pews, was a much greater temptation in the comfort of a living-room.

Worship at home was also subject to many influences which did not affect public worship. There were often technical distractions, because the usefulness of a broad cast depended basically on the quality of reproduction Blurred speech, high-pitched music, crackling in the receiver, fading, distortion, and sometimes complete loss of sound in poor reception areas, could result in irritation rather than edification. Even under ideal conditions, there was much to detract from the true spirit of worship – the voice of the broadcaster, his rate of speaking, pauses or the lack of them – all added to the unreality of word or music issuing from an inanimate piece of mechanism. The mood of the individual listener, his ability to understand what he heard, his physical and mental fitness, and the loyalty of his faith – these too had their effect on the value of an act of worship by radio.

At the receiving end in the family circle, still more adjustments had to be made to ensure true worship. To many people accustomed to orthodox forms, especially the old and sick, most of them loyal members of the church who could no longer attend regularly, the words of the announcer or preacher 'Let us worship God', coming

44

to their ears in domestic surroundings, often caused embarrassment and was felt to be a poor substitute for corporate worship in a consecrated building. Again, if there were young children at home, unused to keeping quiet for any length of time, or members of a family or friends, neither anxious to accept religion by radio, nor in the mood for worship, little benefit would result. In a church, such people would at least try to appear attentive, however much their minds might wander but, in the unrestricted atmosphere of home, they could walk round the room, talk, comment on what was being done, criticise the sermon as it proceeded, and generally reduce the value of the worship for others.

Even the habits and customs of a household could help or hinder the benefit of such broadcasts. If meal-times should clash with radio timings, or children were being put to bed during the transmission; if the broadcast had to compete with other occupations, such as reading or desultory conversation, real worship became impossible, and the loudspeaker provided little more than background noise. Few houses could be so arranged that one room was set aside for this purpose; in practice only those who really desired to share fully in worship by radio were able to make their homes into a sanctuary.

From the early days, it was discovered that some of those listening on Sunday evenings were either on the fringe of organised religion or lapsed members, while others had never been at a church service and had no personal faith. For such, the formality of worship was a limiting factor. The liturgy, so cherished by loyal church people, was quite unfamiliar to them, and responses were little more than a distraction. Studio services were therefore more suitable for such listeners, but it was difficult to label them for a particular category, and more harm than good could result from tuning in to a cathedral service if it could be neither understood nor appreciated.

Religious broadcasting was severely handicapped as an evangelistic force by having to provide for such a complex audience with such varied tastes. Attempts before the war to reach the intellectuals by serious argument, and the indifferent by simple methods of presentation, were only partly successful – indeed, St Martin's with Dick Sheppard and Pat M'Cormack, and St Michael's, Chester Square, with W. H. Elliott, were the only really popular acts of worship broadcast at that period. It is rather ironical to reflect that it was not until the country faced the dangers of modern warfare that new types of worship were introduced to appeal to those outside church membership.

There is a certain mysterious affinity between worship and wireless. To put it in its simplest terms, people wanted to tune in to God's wavelength. As an African Christian expressed it, 'If God can do anything, why does He not broadcast so that we can hear His voice and know how He wants us to live?' The voices of broadcasters received in the homes of listeners without apparent contact seemed to many, especially during the hours of darkness, to come from ethereal realms out of this world. As Jesus said of the wind, 'It bloweth where it listeth', so the Word of God entered into the homes and hearts of those willing to receive it. Distance and time were no barrier; the only criterion was readiness to receive the Word 'in spirit and in truth'. This might seem little more than another form of superstition, but the power of the Spirit of God to guard, guide and comfort was to many a very real experience especially in days of trial and suffering.

In his Lewis Fry lecture of 1948, Sir William Haley, who was Director General of the BBC from 1943 until 1952, spoke of the 'cultural responsibility of the Corporation to join the two extremes (the cultured and uncultured) by a bridge or ladder along which the listener could be induced to progress'. He added that 'this approach rests on the conception of the community as a broadly based cultural pyramid slowly aspiring upwards'. It might almost be said to stretch from Charing Cross to Heaven. In terms of religious broadcasting, its base would be found in the war years in the Sunday Half-Hour of Community Hymn-Singing and, on the next rung, the Forces, later the People's Service and, up one from that level, 'Lift up your hearts', and 'Think on these things'. Higher still, but reached or heard by fewer people, were the Sunday services and talks, and special items for children. It was a fact that the more popular broadcasts were aimed at the public with little or no church connection. Religion out of a box had definite attractions for the uninitiated and the uncommitted. A longing for a simple, practical faith was apparent, and an increasing number of those engaged in the war effort looked to radio to supply it. Worship was next to impossible in crowded huts or barrack rooms, but on isolated gunsites and on ships on patrol in dangerous waters, participation was sincere and meant a great deal to those taking part, as did listening in hospital and sick-room. The audience to such broadcasts could be numbered in millions, many more than attended all the churches in Britain on any Sunday. No accurate assessment of the value of this new approach to worship could be made, and no dramatic increase of church membership was recorded in the immediate post-war period, but there is little doubt that those who listened seriously were at least made familiar with the acts and forms of worship of the different denominations. This vast multitude of home or national service worshippers could not be placed in any recognised category except as men and women in search of a loving God.

The acknowledged aim of the BBC in its religious broadcasts was to make Britain a more Christian country. The Corporation had thus a responsibility for the kind of worship included in its programme schedules, subject to the limitations of the medium. Gradually the most appropriate forms were evolved, and a selection of hymns and prayers was made to meet the need of the majority of both regular and casual listeners. With the help of audience research, the reaction to particular items was known and adjustments made to improve the technique of presentation. It was always recognised that worship by radio could never be a complete substitute for corporate worship, though a number of listeners would be drawn away from public worship. The irony of the situation was that, the better the broadcasts, the more some people would regard going to church as unnecessary, and look to broadcasting to meet the needs of their spiritual life. Church leaders were naturally concerned about this consequence of worship by radio, but were consoled by the fact that, if few conversions and new loyalties were recorded, such listeners would at least know a good deal more about Christian worship.

The most intimate acts of worship are the sacraments. As has already been noted, the recommendation to the BBC whether to permit or refuse the broadcasting of Holy Communion was one of the most difficult CRAC had to make, first in sound radio, and later in television. Apart from the propriety of indiscriminate listening to such a corporate and yet intensely individual act of worship, it seemed quite impossible to transmit this sacrament in all its reverence and dignity. That was the feeling of Mr Reith when the question was first raised in 1923 – his comment being that the BBC had neither the intention nor the desire to broadcast the mystery of the Sacrament of Holy Communion. This view was confirmed and reaffirmed from time to time but, in 1932, on the occasion of a Eucharistic Congress in Dublin, an exception was made and Pontifical High Mass was relayed from Phoenix Park in that city. Five years later, however, at the Coronation ceremony of King George VI and Queen Elizabeth, which included a celebration of Holy Communion, it was decided after considerable discussion that the actual communion should

be omitted from the broadcast and organ music substituted. The war years brought another exception in the
broadcast of Midnight Mass on Christmas Eve for members
of the Roman Church in the services, but it was some time
after peace was restored before requests from the sick and
invalid members of the Anglican Church made it necessary to reconsider the matter. As a result of much consultation with CRAC, the Episcopal form of the Communion Service was broadcast as an experiment on six
occasions during 1946. A devotional commentary was
included, and it was regarded as 'a means of presenting
the faith and practice of the Christian Church more
completely'. This was done in the full realisation that to
overhear or to eavesdrop on such an intimate experience
could result in feelings of apprehension, disappointment
or frustration, or even derision. To those who knew and
loved the service, it became a wonderful spiritual occasion,
reviving tender memories of 'blessed moments on the
Mount', but to others unfamiliar with the 'action', it engendered either a wistful longing to know more about it,
or a critical disregard for its reverence and sanctity, possibly drawing some back into the church but turning
others away from it. This risk had to be taken; in practice
the experiment was fully justified.

The consequence of broadcasting Holy Communion on
sound radio was that it should also be televised. If the
problems of being able to make this service available for
listeners were considerable, they were greatly increased
by television, both for those making the technical and
presentation arrangements, and for viewers in their own
homes. Distance was eliminated, and the whole action of
the consecration and partaking became as clearly visible
at home as to those in church directly receiving the
symbols of bread and wine. The risks of irreverence were
far greater than when hearing only and, for the sick and
housebound, many of them loyal church members, there

was the temptation to make the Sacrament real and com
plete by taking similar elements to those used in face o
the congregation, and partake in private or in the family
circle. Cases of this kind were reported and, though they
might seem to be sacrilege of a serious nature, there i
sufficient Biblical evidence to show that, in the earlies
days of Christianity, the Communion was a rite of the
home rather than the sanctuary. The Apostles broke bread
from house to house because there were no meeting place
for corporate worship. There was no emphasis on the
consecration and, in those days as today, the effect of the
Sacrament depended on the faith of the communicant.

In television, denominational differences were intensi
fied. The pageant of the Mass of the Roman Church wa
eminently suited for viewing. The Communion of the
Anglican Church could be adapted for the small screen
but the other types of celebration were less suitable, and
ministers of these churches were reluctant to agree to thi
Sacrament being televised. The Methodists preferred an
evening Communion, and objections were raised to specia
celebrations being arranged for broadcast purposes. The
Church of Scotland was at first strongly opposed to such
treatment of their most cherished Sacrament. After the
experimental broadcasts in 1948, however, the Lowe
House of Convocation in England agreed to further relays
and the General Assembly of the Church of Scotland
allowed one service to be televised as an experiment. This
came from Dunbarney Parish Church, Perthshire, and wa
conducted by Dr T. B. Stewart Thomson, an experienced
broadcaster and an early member of the Scottish Religiou
Advisory Committee.

The liturgy of the service of Communion and it
traditional forms were even more sacrosanct than the
Prayer Book to the Anglican Church. The Free churche
had more flexibility, and some surprising variations were
revealed in the radio and television presentation of thei

services. To ensure some general conformity, CRAC recommended that the whole service should be broadcast at the time it was usually celebrated in cathedral or church before a worshipping congregation. This in itself involved technical problems of lighting, camera positions, microphones, and overall control, but the most disturbing effect was the embarrassment of communicants – indeed, those who attended churches selected for televised broadcasts were subjected to much extraneous noise and distraction, making the celebration of less spiritual value for them so that unseen viewers might share in it. In spite of all these difficulties, the experiments enabled the Sacrament of Holy Communion as celebrated by the great denominations of the Christian Church in Britain to be broadcast at regular intervals for the benefit of many who were greatly strengthened by it.

CHAPTER IV

PRAYER IN SECRET

Hearing the Still Small Voice

'When thou prayest – in secret'

Baron von Hugel, the great German mystic, once said that Christianity for every man began on his knees. If this were literally applied, it would mean that only those who knelt at prayer would qualify even to begin to learn the Christian way of life. While many worshippers in this country are accustomed to kneel in prayer, there are many others who pray either sitting or standing with heads bowed and eyes shut, an attitude which makes it difficult to use a prayer book with liturgy and rubrics. When in addition to these variations in practice, the place of prayer is transferred from churches to a multitude of homes, a very different reaction may be expected when the familiar words 'Let us pray' are heard by radio. To assume the kneeling posture may take much courage among family or friends, unless the habit of the household is to pray together regularly – a practice to be found in very few homes in this generation. Even 'in secret' in the privacy of one's own room, the posture adopted will depend on whether the custom of the individual at prayer agrees with the directions from outside. And when the person is confined to bed, kneeling becomes impracticable. There must be some modification of von Hugel's assertion so far as listening is concerned. It follows that prayer as part of religion by radio has its peculiar problems.

True prayer has been defined as 'the communion of

52

man with the living personal God', and history has recorded almost infinite variety in man's attempts to establish this contact with God. To speak to an Unseen God in an audible voice is for some people an embarrassing experience, especially in isolation. Archbishop Temple once said that if he were given only five minutes for prayer, he would listen for four, and speak for one. So true prayer in secret in the quiet of one's own room postulates a new approach. The radio audience must learn to listen in silence, and adopt the attitude of 'prayerful listening'.

There are, however, obvious advantages for many people in being freed from the distractions and disciplines associated with corporate prayer – the intoning of the service, responses, and strict adherence to a liturgy. In theory the prayerful listener should be able to establish contact with God, share in the prayers offered, and so become part of a great fellowship of men and women at prayer bound together by a deep common urge. The scripture injunction, 'When ye pray, go into a room by yourself, shut the door, and pray to your Father who is there in the secret place' may be easy or difficult to achieve under modern conditions. In practice, when the secrecy is invaded by strange voices, we will accept them in the selfish hope that they will help us to express our urgent particular needs to God and, if these are not met, we are inclined to become impatient.

With the vast radio audience in mind, how could those who led the prayers broadcast hope to satisfy such varied – and often apparently selfish – wants and direct this huge volume of traffic to heaven? The great prayers of the church provided the answer, but the ignorant and un-initiated would require help to understand them and make them real. This in itself created a dilemma. Could non-liturgical prayers be used without incurring justifiable criticism from those who regarded the Prayer Book as approved by Parliament to be the only correct method of approach to God? The difficulty was solved in broadcasts from churches using the form of prayer practised in these buildings, but ministers of the Free Churches in England and of the Church of Scotland, as well as of evangelical bodies that might be offered broadcasts, used extempore prayer as their normal practice, though usually based on the broad divisions of the Prayer Book. The BBC was chiefly concerned that prayers should be short and simple, and did not encourage discursive or 'preaching' prayers – like the old Scottish divine who began a long prayer with the words, 'Paradoxical as it may seem, O Lord'.

In services from the studio more supervision was possible. The same general rules applied – brevity, simplicity, directness, with appropriate collects. There was increasing need, however, for definite guidance for clergy chosen to broadcast, not for the sake of conformity but to help them to meet the requests of so many earnest listeners. The booklet *Services for Broadcasting*, to guide those leading worship, included prayers for use at the great Christian festivals on such varied subjects as The Kingship of Christ, Fatherly Care, Home and Friendship, Health, Recreation and Healing, Business and Industry, and Avenues of the Spirit. It was a first attempt to unite in prayer and worship the men behind the microphone with listeners who were trying to satisfy their religious need by radio.

When the Daily Service was started with experimental broadcasts, those who heard it were invited to suggest subjects for prayer. Within a month, some 8,000 letters were received with many requests for prayers for special and particular needs. In the fifteen minutes allotted to this item, there was time for two short prayers, including simple confession, thanksgiving, and petition, and the Lord's Prayer. As the service became established, the clergymen who officiated anonymously collected the most uitable prayers and, in December 1928, a booklet entitled *This Day* was published for use in this broadcast. Dick Sheppard wrote an introduction and referred to the compiler, Hugh Johnston, Vicar of Cranleigh, as one who had had a unique experience in that he had led thousands of people in prayer each day and, from contact with them, had come to realise what prayers would be most appreciated. It was stressed that *This Day* was not a service book of the BBC, but a collection prepared for the assistance of those who were increasingly in need of 'what seems real to them' as against the archaic and unreal. Couched in simple, direct, non-theological language, the prayers were grouped in a variety of subjects – for those sick or in trouble, home, children and absent friends, international and national life, the more abundant life, Christian work in all lands, the church universal, the work of the church, and those carrying on the world's work. Drawn from many sources old and new, they served the purpose of helping listeners to make articulate their thoughts and aspirations. The book ran into several editions until a new version was published in 1932 with the title *Where Two or Three*. Its contents were grouped round the general theme of the Lord's Prayer with five sections – Our Father, Hallowed be Thy Name, Thy Kingdom Come, Thy Will be Done, and Lead Us. As before, it was much in demand and must have enabled many thousands of listeners to share more fully in the Daily Service. It also aimed at leading any who had used *This Day* to take a further step in the practice of personal prayer, so making it easier for them to express their secret longings and desires to God.

The publication of *Where Two or Three* coincided with the opening of a religious studio in Broadcasting House in London. The first Daily Service was conducted there by Pat M'Cormick, who included appropriate prayers for those who would use the studio. He prayed for the welfare of those who might listen – 'to know God near as friend,

encourager, and guide, that they might have a real sense
of fellowship with Him and one another, so that they
might know the companionship of prayer'. Thus a regular
congregation of daily worshippers was built up, ready to
respond to true prayer. How and where they listened
mattered little compared with their sincerity and longing
to keep in vital contact with God. The uniqueness of the
Daily Service for more than thirty years has been the simplicity and direct helpfulness of the prayers. Regular
listeners were able to put into practice the poet's familiar
lines:

> 'Here in a quiet room
> Pause for a little space,
> And without faithless gloom,
> With joy upon thy face,
> Pray for God's grace.'

The Book of Common Prayer was used in the weekly
Evensong from Wesminster Abbey broadcast on Thursday
afternoon. This was a fully liturgical service, the only
deviation from the Prayer Book being in the reading,
often taken from the Oxford calendar and lectionary
edited by Dr Percy Dearmer.

In 1936 the BBC took responsibility for the publication
of another book of prayers, *New Every Morning*, for use
in the Daily Service but also available for other occasions.
It was the result of some eighteen months' work by Dr
Iremonger and a small committee of different denominations, except the Roman Catholic, and tried to meet many
requests for a collection of prayers fuller and more varied
than any yet in use. In a foreword, Archbishop Lang wrote
'It gives a stimulus of variety both in the subjects and in
the use of words in the prayers. It expresses the truth that
prayer and supplication should always be accompanied by
thanksgiving. Its intercessions have a singularly wide range
and are themselves an education in the true scope of
Christian prayer, and in the breadth of sympathy and

remembrance which ought to mark the Christian mind'. He commended the inclusion of the old familiar collects of the Prayer Book – 'their quietness, their reverent reserve, the beauty of their rhythm and language when they come in the midst of other prayers longer, more eloquent, more expressive of the thoughts and needs of our modern life'. The book was divided into services for thirty days, and each day followed generally the same pattern – praise and thanksgiving, prayers for the wider needs of humanity, and petitions for individual blessings. It also included a listener's prayer, perhaps the first of its kind ever printed for regular use. It is worth quoting in full.

'Eternal God, who through Thy Holy Spirit art everywhere present, calling us though we hear Thee not, and abiding with us though we know Thee not; we praise Thee for the wonder of Thy universe. We thank Thee for the wisdom of scientists and the skill of craftsmen, whereby its secret forces become servants of the spirit of man. Grant that all who broadcast may use these forces in Thy service, and that no word or sound may fall from them unfit for present needs or unworthy of their calling. And we ask that both they and all who hear may be led in the way of truth, love and beauty to Thee, the Author and Giver of all that is good, through Jesus Christ our Lord.'

The book was widely used by listeners, and proved an inestimable boon to the house-bound, and those in hospital or sick-room, who longed to enter into the secret place of prayer and worship.

During the stresses of war there was need for special and appropriate prayers. Dr Iremonger therefore prepared a selection, taken mostly from *New Every Morning*, for use in these critical times. He chose the title *Each Returning Day* from John Keble's hymn, and explained in the preface that he had compiled the book for worshippers at the Daily Service, for those willing to take trouble over their private prayers, for ministers of religion who wanted to use special intercessions, and for those who had retained or would revive the custom of family prayers. Again there were services for a month, and the subjects included were suitable for all who desired a spiritual link with family or friends in days of separation and anxiety 'arranged in the kind of grouping that makes their use easy for ordinary persons'.

When peace returned, a revised edition of *New Every Morning* became necessary and it was prepared by Eric Fenn in consultation with the staff of the religion department, of which he had become a member some years earlier. Archbishop Fisher wrote a foreword as his predecessor, Archbishop Lang, had done for the first edition, and commended its use as an aid to prayer and worship. In addition to services for a month's use, there were intercessions for a week, collects, and additional prayers for special occasions. The daily themes were grouped round the basic tenets of the faith – The Eternal Father, the Divine Son, the Holy Spirit, the Blessed Trinity, the Christian life, and the Pattern Prayer. It was hoped that the book might be used in services broadcast from churches as well as in the studio, but there was little evidence of this, though some of the collects and prayers were often heard in worship and came into general use.

There were still many listeners either unable or unwilling to share in the prayers at the Sunday or daily services. And yet they needed the help prayer could give to overtired workers, harassed industrialists and business men, weary housewives, the sick, aged and infirm. In prayer at what may be called the 'lower levels', contact with God is possible anywhere and at any time, not only in a sacred building, but in the rough and tumble of life, at home, at work or play, amid the noise of traffic or machinery, in the rush and bustle of shopping, tending children or cooking for a family. It was more difficult for radio to cater for such categories and, in the pre-war years, little consideration was given to these busy and needy people. It was during the emergency that a few minutes were set apart before ten o'clock each morning in the Forces Programme for 'a story, a hymn, and a prayer'. Later the People's Service on Sunday was designed for them and, as we have seen, attracted an audience numbered in millions.

It is obvious that ejaculatory and spontaneous prayer is not easily adaptable to the technique of the microphone. An attempt was made when the war crisis was at its height and the nation was in dire peril to express in prayers broadcast at the close of the day thoughts and petitions for the safety of loved ones and absent friends, and these were much appreciated. Another helpful suggestion was to use the minute that Big Ben took to strike nine o'clock before the news bulletin for prayer. Thoughts of those in danger, dedication to the victory of righteousness and freedom, and earnest prayers for peace could be included. It was also found that the sentences of the Lord's Prayer could be fitted into the strikes of Big Ben, and this brought comfort and hope to many.

H. G. Wells once wrote that thousands of people were unable to sleep because of fear. He was not a specially religious man, but what better antidote to fear than prayer to a loving God? The Epilogue on Sunday nights was one way of achieving this, but it contained no actual prayers. The Silent Fellowship – a curious title for an item heard in sound radio – also aimed at soothing and comforting those unable to sleep. It was a fellowship without formal enrolment or rules, and was presented from Wales at the end of the Sunday evening programme by E. R. Appleton, the Station Director. It was a devotional item for the sick and weary of body and mind to give them calm and solace in the quiet of their homes. It also gave an opportunity for the healthy to think of the suffering by joining in prayer for them, and uniting listeners in pleading with God on behalf of needy humanity.

W. H. Elliott used his popularity to build a League of Prayer for peace when the clouds of war were gathering in the thirties. The senior League had 350,000 members, and the junior some 10,000 mainly school children. When they joined, they were issued with a prayer which they promised to use every day. Reunion meetings were held in the Albert Hall, and it was evident that a very wide unity of common interest had been formed round a broadcast service. Its defect was that it was bound to a person rather than to a continuing organisation.

The recurring problem was how far radio could be used to instruct listeners in the practice of prayer. Perhaps the publication of collections of prayers for use at the microphone was all that the limitations of the medium would permit, and the attitude of the churches to liturgical and extempore prayer gave little encouragement. Yet it would seem that the BBC had missed a unique opportunity to provide instruction and give guidance to those who anxiously wanted to learn about prayer as a power and strength for daily living, and to many others looking for a quiet prayerful ending to this mortal life. Over the years numerous talks were broadcast on every aspect of prayer, and the best were printed in *The Listener*, but a School of Prayer was never formed to give definite and detailed teaching which radio supplied for so many other activities of our social and national life. If it had been possible to translate into simple modern terms the example and devotion of the saints as they wrestled with God in prayer, the BBC might have enrolled many sincere, earnest people willing and ready to learn that God is always at hand to hear even the merest whisper and that, by quiet expectant listening, they could recognise His 'still small voice' speaking to them and inviting them to enter into 'the secret place of the Most High'.

CHAPTER V

BROADCAST PRAISE

Pæans of Praise to God

'Glory to God in the Highest'

The Bible is shot through with song and praise to the glory of God. The Old Testament has a vast and varied collection of sacred song (for that is the meaning of psalm), and many great pæans of praise. The New Testament opens with the song of the angels at the birth of Jesus, and ends with the songs of the redeemed in heaven.

Praise is one of the most satisfying ways of expressing reverence and emotion. Popular hymns and sacred music can evoke deep feeling and strengthen faith. It was natural that the BBC should use this effective means of communicating religion. There was, however, some initial delay in introducing praise into religious programmes. The short address broadcast on Sunday evening during the first year of radio was often sandwiched between works of secular music – indeed the first studio broadcast by Dick Sheppard in July 1923 was preceded by the Band of the Royal Air Force playing 'In a Monastery Garden', and was followed by a band version of the hymn 'Fight the Good Fight'. In due course, a sung hymn was included and, when reading and prayer were added, it became an act of worship. In the service relayed from St Martin's early in 1924, the praise consisted of popular hymns without canticles or anthem, somewhat different from the usual Anglican custom, perhaps because Dick Sheppard had expressed doubts about the musical standards of his choir. At this period, provincial stations broadcast more services of traditional type than London. It is surprising to note that so little praise in the Sunday programme came from the metropolis in these days.

Other items of religious praise, however, found their way on to the air. A talk on the old Scottish psalm tunes, with illustrations by the choir of St Columba's (Church of Scotland) in London, was given by Dr Archibald Fleming in June 1924, and that great and beloved musician, Sir Walford Davies, was reported to have given a talk on 'The Function of Praise in Worship' at a World Educational Conference in Edinburgh, though it was not broadcast. About the same time, a long series on famous hymns and their story was featured in *Radio Times*, thus creating an interest in sacred praise for the microphone. Handel's *Messiah* was first presented for radio from a studio in London in November 1924, with Dorothy Silk, Astra Desmond, Rex Palmer, and John Coates as soloists. Its regular inclusion as 'an inseparable part of the Christmas season' dated from a performance in York in 1928. Other sacred works had been broadcast, beginning at Easter 1926 with the St Matthew Passion from York, the cantata *Gethsemane* with verse by John Masefield from Birmingham and, a few months later, the annual festival of parochial choirs, with a programme of psalms, canticles, hymns and anthems, from Canterbury Cathedral. The use of church choirs to present the great music of the Christian tradition had been brought into the service of radio and, if the Sunday services lacked these magnificent expressions of sacred praise, they were made available for listeners at other times.

The regular broadcasts of the complete series of Bach cantatas on Sunday afternoons began in 1928. They had been described as 'the supreme contribution of art to the protestant religion' and, after they had been presented for a year without any alternative item, Filson Young wrote

in *Radio Times* that they had fulfilled the prophecy of
being 'more wonderful and stimulating artistically than
any other work of Bach'. Some listeners were less en-
thusiastic about the length of the series, and one corres-
pondent sent a letter which was published in *Radio Times*
to the effect that people were tired of 'an overdose of Bach
cantatas'. The story was also told of the taxi-driver who,
when hired by a musician at Euston station to be driven
to Broadcasting House, hesitated and then asked whether
he was engaged in 'them Bach cantatas' and, when informed that he was playing the violin in their performance,
he was told that he could just walk. The series lasted some
four years, and certainly provided a great musical and
religious experience for the enlightened music-lover but,
for the majority of the listening public unable to appreciate
fully the musical quality of the broadcasts, it became a
much disliked item without any alternative. The BBC had
not yet learned the importance of ending a series before
people became satiated and critical.

The need for well-sung praise at the Daily Service
resulted in the formation in the early thirties of a group
of professional singers employed by the Corporation.
Though only twelve voices, they were so carefully blended
and rehearsed by their Chorus Master, Leslie Woodgate,
that they set a new standard in sacred praise of great value
to church choirs. The Wireless Singers, as they were called,
led the praise at the daily and studio services, and the
Sunday Epilogue, and helped much to make these intimate
acts of worship of universal appeal.

The choice of hymns for broadcasts raised some practical
questions. What hymn-book should be used in giving the
numbers in the order of service published in *Radio Times*?
Some preferred 'Songs of Praise' as containing a better
selection than 'Ancient and Modern', but in Scotland the
Revised Church Hymnary had been published and contained many hymns found in both books. Broadcasts from

cathedrals and churches followed the practice of quoting numbers and tunes in use in these buildings in the hope that the hymns chosen and the tunes to which they were sung would be familiar or at least known to many of those hearing them. So far as *Radio Times* was concerned, it became the custom to give the hymn numbers in 'Ancient and Modern', 'Songs of Praise', or the 'English Hymnal', as well as the book used in the denomination relaying the service. Even this was sometimes of doubtful value because the number and order of the verses varied from one book to another, and the fact that the words were also different in the versions and books in use caused both irritation and confusion to those following them at home. Added to this, variations in harmony and bad scoring of the tunes in some books, together with the emphasis on prose psalms in England and on metrical psalms in Scotland, reduced the musical and spiritual value of the praise for those steeped in the traditions of their churches. So long as the BBC was eavesdropping on worship in church, a solution was far from easy to find.

In the early thirties the need of a hymn book for broadcast purposes became as insistent as the lack of suitable collections of prayers ten years before for use in daily and studio services. A committee was set up by the Corporation in 1937 to make a selection of hymns for broadcasting. Dr Iremonger suggested that 'good popular' might be preserved and 'bad popular' might be discarded. The great hymns of the church would be included and enriched by a number of new ones not found in most of the standard books. It was to have a wide and inclusive appeal. The members of the committee were to make a critical study of the hymns most frequently used in the worship of the denominations and to recommend the most suitable for the new book. In this way, a list of some 500 hymns was compiled and sent for comment to eminent hymnologists and musicians. The work of preparation had to be

suspended on the outbreak of war, but another committee, under the chairmanship of Sir Hugh Allen, was
appointed in 1941 to complete the book, and it was finally
published in 1950. The result was a collection of 542
hymns, divided into sections dealing with God as the
Eternal Father; the Lord Jesus Christ and the Holy Spirit;
the Church of God; the Christian life and duty; times;
seasons and occasions; Metrical Psalms; Bible Paraphrases;
and choir settings. There was no section of general hymns
as in most other books but, in addition to those for use in
studio services, some of the Communion hymns, and others
for baptism, confirmation, and marriage were included to
make the book suitable for ordinary church worship.
Many copies were sold, but there was little evidence that
it superseded the long-established collections. It received
much appreciative comment from music critics, choir-
masters, and those who took the trouble to use it when
listening to services, the Sunday Half-hour, and other
items of sacred praise. Great credit was due to Cyril
Taylor, then a member of the religion department of
the BBC, for his careful editorial work and fine music
contributions.

Good congregational singing was essential for successful
outside broadcasts, but cathedrals and churches with professional choirs often failed to get worshippers to join in
the praise. Their singing was generally of a high standard,
as was found in the Choral Evensong on Thursday afternoons, but it was the parish and amateur choirs that could
be relied upon to provide hearty, if not always very har-
monious and balanced, congregational praise. As was to
be expected, Welsh choirs and Salvation Army choristers
excelled in making others join in hymn singing. They
knew how to praise the Lord with 'mirth' as the psalmist
directed. In the thirties, carolares were a regular Sunday
afternoon item from Wales, and became a forerunner of
the Sunday Half-hour in the war years.

E

Another essential for satisfactory listening was good technical reception. In relays from churches the BBC engineers, many of them without any training in music, made every effort to reproduce the atmosphere of reverent worship, with the audible participation of the congregation in praise and responses. To 'balance' a choir was the work of an expert musician, but lack of staff resulted in many outside broadcasts being controlled by technicians whose careful preparations, which were to them a labour of love rather than just another assignment, made the relays often more acceptable to the average listener than the studio services with their professional music control. A recital by the choir, however good, was not wanted; a sincere spirit of worship was preferred – that mysterious sense of reverence and reality that made those listening feel that they were actually sharing in the service.

The Sunday Half-hour of Community Hymn Singing was begun in wartime for troops and civilians who might want to join in this act of corporate praise. It was broadcast at eight-thirty in the evening in the Forces Programme and, as we have already seen, had an audience numbered in millions. 'Think on these things', a meditation on familiar hymns later in the evening, attracted nearly as many listeners. While the selection of hymns for these items was rather limited and lacked variety, the value of this type of praise was that many of the hymns, already well known to church people, came to be sung by those with little or no church connection. How much the singing of massed choirs inspired listeners to lift up their voices in song in their own homes, or in barrack, camp or ship will never be known, but there is no doubt that such items performed a useful function, and brought comfort and strength to countless people facing danger, suffering and even death in these terrible years. They continued to exercise a rich ministry in the postwar period. Sacred praise had given to radio a new method of reaching receptive hearts

However popular the appeal of community hymn singing, the finest work of choirs and choral societies was not
forgotten, and made an increasing contribution over the
years. As already mentioned, Handel's *Messiah* became a
regular feature at Christmas. At other seasons, the well-
known oratorios – and some not so well known – found
their place. Outstanding among these was the Festival of
Nine Lessons and Carols from King's College, Cambridge,
on Christmas Eve. It had been designed by a Dean of the
College early in the century, based on a traditional service
in Truro Cathedral, and expressed in simple and appropriate readings with carols the spirit of Christmas. It has become a regular and deeply moving item of celebration at
that season. The annual Festival of Three Choirs from
Gloucester, Hereford, and Worcester was another distinctive combination of chorus, orchestra, and organ,
offered in rotation from these fine buildings with a real
atmosphere of worship, acoustics admirably suited to the
works performed, and sensitive and inspired rendering of
sacred music. A different aspect of broadcast praise was
demonstrated when Sir Walford Davies introduced and
directed a series of recitals on the 'Melodies of Christendom', which he described as 'A half-hour of quiet loveliness'
from music composed for the church over the centuries.

Many other series and recitals helped to swell the
volume of praise, and often they were to be found in
unusual places on week-days as well as on Sundays. Choirs
such as the famous Glasgow Orpheus generally included a
hymn or psalm in its concerts and in the course for schools,
'Singing Together', in carol and carillon recitals, and even
in community singing at international football matches,
familiar hymns were heard. The result was that, at every
stage of social and Christian influence, sacred praise re-
sounded over the air and entered thousands of homes,
making people conscious as never before of the wealth of
our hymnology, with its collections of hymns, psalms,

anthems, canticles, cantatas, and oratorios. An almost ethereal feeling was created by hearing the pure treble voice of a boy chorister in a carol from Cambridge, or the Hallelujah Chorus from the *Messiah* sung by the Huddersfield Choral Society, not to mention the faultless intonation of the Wireless Singers. Few could listen to these acts of praise without being moved. Broadcasting had made sacred praise popular. Hymns known only to the few became common currency in workshop and factory as well as in hospital and home. Standards of choir and choral singing were appreciably raised by hearing the finest renderings of works by the great composers. The climax came in the music of the Coronations in 1937 and 1953, heard by millions all over the world, a magnificent pæan of praise to Almighty God.

Television has continued to provide items of sacred praise, choral works, and popular hymns. The Sunday Half-hour has been adapted for the screen as 'Songs of Praise', and a request programme 'Rejoice and Sing' for a time alternated with it. Much careful preparation and artistic presentation was required to make choir or choral singing attractive to viewers, but difficulties were overcome by experience, and the reaction to sincere reverent praise at televised services and on other occasions has made as great an impact as was felt by listeners before television began. Singing praises to God by radio can indeed stir deep emotions, lead to a firmer faith, and strengthen spiritual life.

CHAPTER VI

PREACHING WITHOUT PULPIT

Hearing and Understanding the Word

'Necessity is laid on me – to preach'

Religious broadcasting began with preaching, using that word in a special sense. The short address from the studio on Sunday evenings was hardly a preachment, neither was it a sermon; it was rather a kind of homily or fireside talk. *Radio Times* published for some years a feature called 'The Broadcast Pulpit' giving excerpts from these addresses. They were for the most part intimate and personal rather than public proclamations of the Gospel. Read from prepared scripts, their effect was produced, not by great eloquence, but by the persuasive voices of the speakers. Their brevity influenced the style of writing and speaking, and the restricted conditions of the early studios, draped with thick curtains and without any immediate audience reaction, made sermons seem unreal and artificial. To most preachers, it entailed a radical change in their usual mode of speech. Gestures and mannerisms simply had no meaning, but the proper inflection of the voice, short sentences, good phrasing, and carefully regulated pauses were of prime importance. It was a novel experience for all who took part in it, and demanded a new technique. Dr

Archibald Fleming put it well when he wrote in *Radio Times*, 'Virtue must go out of the preacher, as from heart to heart, mind to mind, and soul to soul. His pulse must respond to his unseen hearers', and J. W. Robertson Scott summed up the requirements of such preaching as 'heartfelt manly utterance, tones as unlike the clerical as they could be, words spoken with complete earnestness and sincerity, brotherly talk of honest, thinking, humble-minded men, simple phrases of experience and hope, faith and conviction, speech without dogma, full of charity, liberality, and inspiration'.

Viewed over the span of the years, the question immediately arises, was this preaching? The Oxford dictionary includes a religious address in its definition, but the Reformation had emphasised the sermon as the proclamation of the Word and, in varying degree, the Reformed Churches had made preaching based on a text of scripture a central act of their worship. How was this tradition and practice to fit into the needs of radio? Relays from cathedrals and churches followed the pattern of worship and preaching normally in use there, except that strict timing was essential, and the preacher had to realise that his unseen audience could not be held attentive by dramatic gestures or rhetoric. One of the early complaints to the Advisory Committee in Manchester was that sermons were given with too much pulpit delivery, instead of being simple and intimate. It became apparent that radio required a new approach to preaching. In the Gospels, the primary function of Christ's ministry was to preach. He came to proclaim the message of God's love for mankind, the word of authority from God to man. Ministers of religion had laid upon themselves the privilege and responsibility of continuing that proclamation. As St Paul expressed it, 'Necessity is laid upon me; woe is unto me if I preach not the Gospel.' In these modern times, as of old, the preacher delivers the message and seeks a response from his hearers. F. W. Boreham, the Australian writer, described a preacher as 'an ambassador, a witness, a prophet, and a herald, all in one'.

How many men of this kind were to be found in the pulpits of Britain? As has already been indicated, the selection of clergymen to broadcast was one of the main tasks of the advisory committees. At the very first meeting of CRAC, a list of preachers was drawn up, and some thirty ministers were recommended to be invited to give the Sunday address. A leaflet was prepared, 'Hints to Speakers', as a guide to those chosen to broadcast. It contained the following instructive paragraph:

'You are asked to remember your vast audience is not a crowd or a congregation, but a variety of individuals to whom you are speaking in the intimacy of their homes. This is the audience to be kept in mind. The tone of voice found to have most appeal is that of the intimate and sympathetic talk rather than that of the public address. The address should be framed on different lines from a public speech, and particularly so from an ordinary sermon. In effect, you must not take either the interest or knowledge of your listeners for granted. It is, therefore, wise to introduce the address in a human way, to treat it conversationally, and to avoid as far as possible technical terms not understood by the general listener. It should be remembered that listeners are able to stop listening at will, and thousands of them will switch off their sets if the opening is unattractive.'

Preachers had thus ample information about the technique of speaking at the microphone, but the question still remained, what were they to preach? What message were they to deliver? In such a new medium, those giving broadcast addresses naturally kept to the essential themes of the Gospel, but even this failed to please the critics who complained that their doctrine was watered down, their preaching was anaemic and their exhortations confined almost to the generalisation 'be good and you will be happy'. Some took refuge in platitude, because they felt it to be almost an impertinence to try to meet the individual spiritual need of the unknown millions who might be hearing or overhearing. The dilemma they faced was that what would bring comfort and solace to the sick and aged might have just the opposite effect on many others whose need of good preaching was far greater than the captive audience of the housebound.

The BBC was reluctant to instruct preachers on the theme and subject of their sermons, and they were left with little more than the advice of Mr Reith in the early twenties 'to preach a manly religion'. Dr F. W. Norwood of the City Temple used the opportunity of radio to give the foundations of his belief. 'If I had only sermon to preach, and wanted to epitomise my faith, I would state it boldly, crudely, without qualifying clauses.' He ended his sermon with : 'The love of God releases the power of the spirit. There is only one name for this. It is a Gospel of God's good tidings. Nothing else has touched the deep need of man like that.' This was positive preaching of the love of God for man. Not all broadcast sermons were so forceful and direct, but most of them at least appealed to many of their huge audience. The bread of the Word was being cast upon the waters by radio.

The pioneering years saw much experiment and progress. Men with real gifts were tried out at the microphone, and gradually a group was formed with the personality and ability required for good broadcast preaching. Dick Sheppard was the first of a long line of famous radio preachers who quickly acquired the technique, and attracted larger audiences than had ever been known throughout the Christian centuries. One of the most notable in the pre-war period was W. H. Elliott, who when he first broadcast was Vicar of Holy Trinity, Folkestone, and who later became Rector of St Michael's, Chester Square, London, and a Canon of St Paul's Cathedral. He was one of the first to give a series of addresses on Thursday evenings in 1928. About the same time, on Sunday evenings, Eric Southam, who was then at Bournemouth gave a connected series of three addresses with the title, 'God and Jesus Christ', and sub-titles, 'What is God Like?', 'God and the World's Plan', and 'God in Everyday Life'. A booklet by the Bishop of Winchester giving information about the series was published while the sermons were being broadcast and had a wide circulation focusing attention on a vital theme. The benefit of such a method was that the audience might be induced to listen to the whole series. The disadvantage was that those who missed one sermon might not turn on their sets for the others. This was to some extent obviated by printing excerpts in *The Listener* when it began publication in 1928, and was the sequel to the broadcast pulpit in *Radio Times* some years earlier.

The difference between the studio sermon and that preached in a church before a congregation remained a point for preference and argument. For the loyal church member unable to worship regularly with others, the familiar service with the sermon delivered in resonant pulpit tones was a moving and uplifting experience, but to those unaccustomed to the atmosphere of a sacred building, the more intimate and conversational type of sermon from the studio made a deeper impression. There was a very real difference for the preacher; in church he had two audiences to consider, and there was a danger that he might fail to impress either. In practice it meant that his seen audience had to be sacrified to some extent for the larger unseen number of listeners, linked by science rather than by sight, but able to be united by the spirit of true worship. It was found that those gathered together were, by their very presence, of great assistance in giving the preacher an immediate reaction to his sermon and helping to convey that mysterious spiritual reality which could make radio so effective.

Preachers chosen to face the microphone with or without a congregation had to accustom themselves to reading their sermons – to some a very troublesome exercise especially when their material had to be prepared some weeks in advance of the actual broadcast. In Scotland, where extempore preaching was a recognised custom, this proved a most difficult condition. A famous Edinburgh minister confessed when he was invited to preach on the wireless that he had never before in his whole ministry written a sermon fully and broadcasting was quite foreign to him if it meant reading strictly from a manuscript. But the necessity for keeping to a time schedule, however irritating to the Scottish tradition of long extempore sermons based on a text, made careful timing and advance preparation essential if the worship of God was not to be rudely cut off for some secular item.

In 1938, Dr Iremonger issued some useful hints to preachers about the composition and content of broadcast sermons to counteract the criticisms made against radio preaching. He counselled them not to use abstract words like fellowship, incarnation, justification, which would be quite unintelligible to most listeners. He warned them against being sentimental on the one hand, and too hearty on the other, thus lacking any challenge. He emphasised the ability of the preacher to communicate his message and his ultimate task to make God real to man and to beseech man to be reconciled to God. Then, and only then, could the preaching of the Word be an effectual means of converting sinners, and of building them up in holiness and faith unto salvation. These hints supplemented the booklet of some ten years earlier and helped to establish the broadcast sermon as preaching in its own right.

What a galaxy of famous men have adorned the radio

pulpit over the years! Archbishops, cardinals, bishops, and other clergymen, moderators and ministers, rabbis and brethren – all added to the casting abroad of the seed of the Word into the field of the world and, like the parable of the sower, it fell upon almost infinite quality of ground in those who listened. The themes of the sermons were also very varied, but there was one which occurred again and again – the love of God for man, and man's need of that love as revealed in Jesus Christ. A study of the excerpts printed in *Radio Times* and *The Listener* show an interesting development conditioned by the customs and circumstances of the times. In the twenties, a text of scripture was generally used to announce the theme, and many sermons seemed to reflect the false optimism of that decade. In the thirties, the American practice of starting with a dramatic story or statement became quite normal and applied the comforts of the Christian Gospel to the severe depression and dire poverty of that period. Series of connected addresses were also used to attract and retain the unseen audience. The stresses of war combined these preaching techniques, so that their influence helped to confirm and strengthen faith.

Limitations of policy had their effect on preaching as in other broadcasts. Controversial questions and dogma were excluded and no proselytising was permitted. This tended to reduce preaching to a comfortable presentation of the Christian message and resulted in sermons that could soothe and inspire but rarely convert. The war brought the necessary corrective. A new kind of radio preacher became popular and personalities who could communicate the Gospel were built up. The year books of the BBC, which published lists of outstanding speakers, gave a cross-section of preachers of every denomination whose names, though often not well known in church circles, had become household words. It is invidious to mention names but some were such outstanding broadcast preachers that they formed the nucleus of a band of men who had dedicated themselves to this new medium, and were able to speak as convincingly to their vast unseen audience as the great pulpit orators of an earlier generation, who had thrilled those who came together to hear them. The broadcast pulpit would have been much the poorer without such familiar names as Dick Sheppard, Leslie Weatherhead, Eric Southam, Bishop Barnes, Dean Matthews, Donald Soper, George MacLeod and Ronald Selby Wright. They and many others justified preaching without pulpit with its simple presentation of the redeeming love of Christ as true preaching, and gave to radio the power to make religion real to this generation.

CHAPTER VII

TEACHING OUT OF THE AIR

Bible Stories in Every Guise

'When he was set – He taught them'

Public broadcasting began as a business venture to induce people to buy receivers. Entertainment was the main ingredient of the programmes, but other items soon found their way into the schedules – weather reports, news bulletins, and talks on subjects of general interest. Mr Reith, who was General Manager of the Company at that time, justified this policy by describing entertainment as occupying one's leisure hours agreeably. This broad definition included a wide variety of items and, in the first few years, religious talks and stories from the Bible were included but little attempt was made to teach religion by radio.

One of the early experiments in this direction was made in July 1925 in Birmingham, when a series of talks was broadcast on Sunday evenings. They may have been inspired by the Conference on Christian Politics, Economics, and Citizenship, known as COPEC, which had been held in that city. The purpose of the series, which was inter-denominational, was said to be didactic, and the subjects chosen for discussion included the Bible, the Sacraments, the church and the ministry, and theology for the average man – fairly stiff material for summer Sunday listening.

The speakers were two college principals, a professor and a canon of Birmingham Cathedral. Little comment, appreciative or otherwise, was received, and five years passed before another series intended for students and leaders of Bible classes was broadcast from London. It dealt with such topics as the psychology of religion, society and politics in the Old Testament, and the beginnings of Christian theology – again stiff listening even for the initiated.

It was left to the Joint Committee of the Convocation of Canterbury to urge in its Report of 1931 that there should be a teaching element in religious programmes. It was argued that as lectures in science and art were broadcast to whet the appetite for serious study, so instruction in religion might lead to study circles and groups being formed to hear and discuss the talks. The suggestion was supported by the fact that the syllabus for church and council schools was based on the Creed, the Lord's Prayer, and the moral teachings of the Gospels. The BBC was asked to provide 'more scholarly broadcasts' based on this framework for groups and for pupils in schools able to receive them. It is interesting to note that no recommendation along these lines appears to have come from CRAC, but that body gladly acquiesced in this development.

In the early thirties when the novelty of the pioneering days was wearing off, radio in Britain was looking for a new intellectual force to attract and inspire listeners. In contrast to the suspicions of the twenties, help soon came from the churches. A series of talks or lectures was suggested, as the Year Book of 1934 put it, 'to present a definite statement of the ideals and claims of Christianity, and endeavour to show its relevance to the lives of men and women to-day'. This led to important series on the basic beliefs of the faith. The first was broadcast in the autumn of 1932 as an experiment with the general title, 'God in a changing world', and dealt with such subjects as the fact of Christ, the Christian faith in the modern world, and God revealed in Christ. It was a prelude to a longer and more fundamental series, 'God and the world through Christian eyes' which, approved and recommended by CRAC, was broadcast on the national programme which covered the whole of the country on the first and third Sundays of the month. Archbishop Lang introduced the series and the first lecture was delivered by Archbishop Temple, then at York. The speakers were chosen for their intellectual ability, without reference to denominational adherence. The series was divided into four sections, and a booklet was issued giving a synopsis of the lectures, with an introductory essay by Leonard Hodgson, a canon of Winchester, who tried to place Christianity in its true perspective as a world religion, expound its distinctive characteristics, and show how the essential Christian doctrines of the Incarnation, the Atonement, and the Resurrection could lead back to a vision of God in this life and on into eternity. He explained that the lectures were for those who would 'gird up the loins of their minds' and seek to understand the faith that had done so much to mould the civilisation and outlook of the world. The first six talks dealt with God; the second with Christ; the third with 'Man and his World'; and the fourth with Christianity. The whole series reflected the theological climate of the pre-war decade. The lectures were printed in *The Listener* to make them available for further study and, while all the speakers were experts in the subjects allotted to them, mention must be made of the most outstanding contributions. Dr W. R. Matthews, then Dean of Exeter, spoke on 'Why man believes in God', and explained in simple terms man's need of God, and His power to give to those who will trust Him a peace that the world cannot give. Professor H. R. Mackintosh, then Moderator of the General Assembly of the Church of Scotland, lectured on 'Christ and faith in God', and showed how faith in the Son increased our knowledge of God as Father, Friend, and one to be trusted as absolute and eternal love. Another Scottish Minister, Professor Donald Baillie of St Andrews University, gave a brilliant exposition on 'Man and the unseen World', and asserted that at the heart of the universe there was 'something infinitely good and therefore trustworthy'. The last two lectures were given by Father Martindale of the Roman Catholic Church, and Dr W. E. Kirk of Trinity College, Oxford. They dealt with the hope of immortality, and the vision of God, and gave a fine climax to the series. Many letters of sincere appreciation reached the BBC and individual speakers, but there was also considerable criticism because it was felt that most of the talks were above the heads of the average listener. The Corporation had sponsored a new approach to religious thinking in a laudable effort to curb the tendency of preachers to try to please their hearers by vague and soothing sermons. It was suggested, however, that the series had gone too far to the other extreme in presenting a comprehensive statement of the faith, suitable for students and clergy, but beyond the understanding of even interested laymen. As a result, another series recommended by CRAC was planned and broadcast, with the title 'The Way to God'. In his foreword to the attractive pamphlet prepared to make for better appreciation of the talks, Archbishop Temple explained that this series, in contrast to its predecessor, would 'start from the common facts of experience, continue with questions everyone was likely to ask, give the answer the Christian Church exists to proclaim, and end by applying that answer to life and its claim on our attention and action'. He commended the series as providing an excellent opportunity for 'improving the quality of our religious thought'. The talks began from the angle of man with a nature to understand and a life to live related to the One beyond all nature and the source of all life. God and His revelation were then dealt with, leading to a section on the Person and work of Christ and His example for man's life in this world and the next, illustrated from history, and God's power to change and mould the lives of men. The series was an attempt to apply the earlier talks to everyday living and, at the same time, give the most enlightened teaching on our religion which a great English educationist once described as 'that which passes from life, through life, and up to life'.

As before, the speakers were selected for their power to communicate their thoughts and knowledge to others. Dr J. S. Whale of Chestnut College, Cambridge, opened the series and was followed by Dr W. R. Matthews, by now Dean of St Paul's, Father Martindale of the Society of Jesus, Professor C. E. Raven of Cambridge, and Dr George MacLeod of the Iona Community. The arrangement by which each section was allotted to a single speaker enabled continuity to be maintained and the themes to be fully developed. Provision was also made after each section for answers to listeners' questions, and group discussions were encouraged by the inclusion of relevant questions as well as a list of books for study. Again the talks were printed in *The Listener* in the issue following their delivery at the microphone, so that every possible assistance was given to church groups, study circles, and listeners generally to make full use of them. The aim of the series to combine the deep fundamental beliefs of our faith with their practical application to life in this complex age was to a large extent fulfilled. The reaction of the listening public was, however, very mixed, as in the previous series. There was much appreciation from groups and those who took the trouble to listen seriously, but a good deal of comment was again received about the difficulty of full comprehension even after reading the scripts in print. The problem of translating theological terms into everyday spoken language had still to be solved if teaching by radio was to prove effective.

F

The policy of the BBC had been to use the Daventry national programme for religious items with a teaching content, though they were not labelled as such. Sunday afternoons were reserved for children and, from 1926, a children's service was broadcast on the first Sunday of the month, while the others were filled with stories from the Bible, missionary talks, and short dramatic productions on religious themes. The reading of the Scriptures was an obvious method of imparting knowledge and instruction. In 1927, Dr James Moffatt of Bible translation fame, began a series of readings from the Old Testament, dealing with well-known episodes in the lives of such great biblical figures as Abraham, Jacob, and Joseph. They continued for several years and were then replaced by the more popular dramatic presentation of these great stories. Readings were included in broadcasts to schools, using voices appropriate and suitable for the fine language of the Authorised Version. Gradually a group of first-class readers – announcers, clergy, and laymen – was formed, one of whom was the then Director General of the BBC, Lord Reith. This group was able to give inspiration to the words and make Holy Writ real to thousands who heard it read with feeling and understanding. It was said of Dr J. S. Whale that when he read the scripture lessons, there was no need of a sermon. Radio had re-discovered the fact that the Bible, properly read at the microphone, was able to convey its message in a truly remarkable way. These fine broadcast readings were recorded, so that they might be available in more permanent form.

Another way of presenting these stories was tried with success in the early thirties. The Joan and Betty Bible stories originated in Wales. The Cardiff Station Director E. R. Appleton, told them to his daughters as a 'Bible Class' using the resources of radio to make them more vivid. At first offered for local listening, they were later broadcast in the national programme on the second and fourth

Sundays of the month, and continued for some six years.

A teaching group under Dr Basil Yeaxlea of West Hill Training College, Birmingham, arranged many of the other items for children on Sunday afternoons, and brought in people with special aptitude for speaking to children and youth. The broadcasts were popular with both young and older listeners, and succeeded in combining instruction with a measure of entertainment. A kind of radio Sunday School was organised, and made a useful contribution to the religious instruction of youth.

Educational broadcasting had included courses in religion as part of the provision for schools all over Britain in the years before the war. A wide range of material could be presented with the help of expert and informed speakers and all the technical and artistic aids of radio. For younger scholars, the great literature of the Bible and the teaching of Jesus were made available in their classrooms and, for older and sixth-form pupils, courses in theology and comparative religion were provided and filled a need the average school could rarely supply. These were generally accepted by teachers and the public, but other courses to schools, such as biology, although not directly concerned with religion, raised much criticism and resulted in a strong attack on the BBC and the Central Council for School Broadcasting, which sponsored them. In the series 'How things began' and 'Man's place in Nature', the subject of evolution was dealt with from the scientific point of view. These courses were planned to show 'the grand epic of evolution' as it has been called, and described the process of change that had been going on for millions of years to produce the infinite variety of plants and animals that inhabit the earth. But it was never forgotten, as Sir George Adam Smith of Aberdeen University put it, that 'in the proved gradual evolution of the universe and the gradual ascent of man, there is every proof of a Creator'. A number of scientists and humanists formed an Evolutionary Protest Society with little other aim than to ensure that these courses were constantly criticised. It was a facet of the old controversy between science and religion, though it was on scientific rather than on theological grounds that the protests were based. This campaign began before the war, and was renewed after it. The Corporation said that the policy of the series was to deal in the most careful way with the evolution of the human species on the scientific evidence available and consistent with the theological tenets of the faith. Even with this assurance, these school courses came under critical comment from another angle. The Roman Church felt that they disregarded the teaching of that church, and asked that they should not contradict in day schools what was taught elsewhere.

Humanists were active on another front, and continued their pressure on the BBC to permit every statement of religious truth to be contested. The immediate pre-war policy recommended by CRAC was to allow the viewpoint of sceptics to be broadcast without argument, provided there were also speakers to present the Christian attitude. After the war, discussions of widely differing beliefs were permitted, but they had to be presented in such a way that 'they would not wound the feelings of reasonable people, nor transgress the bounds of courtesy and good taste'. Producers on the staff had long felt the limitation of controversial discussion of religious topics as too severe. While perhaps necessary for sermons, it curbed the initiative of speakers, made spontaneous argument impossible, and appear that the Christian faith could not be defended against its critics. As had happened in other aspects of religious output, the regions were more ready to experiment than the programme organisers in London. To encourage listeners to continue arguing after the items, a series of 'Fireside Talks' was broadcast to Scotland as early as 1934, for group or family listening and discussion. Mr Kirk and Mr Walker, fictitious persons representing the extremes of conduct on Sunday, dealt with such current topics as 'Church or no Church', 'Recreation or re-creation on Sundays', 'betting and gambling on any day of the week'. From the same national region, possibly because the Scot is by nature an argumentative person, a series 'Asking them Questions' was broadcast in 1938. These talks were based on the kind of questions members of a boys' club in Edinburgh had asked their leader, Ronald Selby Wright, afterwards the Radio Padre. He persuaded eminent thinkers and theologians to suggest replies to such difficult questions as 'Where is heaven?', 'Does it matter what religion a person has?', 'Did Jesus really rise from the dead?' and 'What is the Holy Spirit?'. The series attracted much attention and was followed by another – 'Youth seeks an answer'. The talks were later published in book form.

One of the great defects of teaching by radio was the fleeting nature of broadcast speech. This was gradually overcome by the help of the printed word. When *The Listener* commenced publication, its official aim was 'to carry home the more serious activities of the microphone in literature, drama and talks, complementary and supplementary to the spoken word, to widen the market of the printed word, and to preserve talks in readable form'. Opportunity was thus made for further study of what had been received by the ear only. This desire for permanency was assisted when the book trade, after refusing to publish anything that had been broadcast, agreed to print talks and series which might sell. In 1934, *The Listener* gave a long list of books on religion and philosophy compiled from broadcasts. It included the series 'God in a Changing World', 'God and the World Through Christian Eyes', a symposium on science and religion, and another on the future life. These were only a small selection of the great variety of talks offered to listeners in the pre-war years.

A perusal of the BBC annuals published at that time and of *Radio Times* provides a comprehensive list of titles. A random sample reveals an emphasis on the impact of the faith on the national and social life of the country in such series as 'The Churches in National Life', 'Christianity and Morals', 'The Validity of Christian Experience', 'The New Christendom of Missionary Achievement', 'The Problem of Evil', 'The Mystery of Pain', 'The Spiritual Life', 'Mysticism', and a series on religious poetry, 'The Pilgrim's Way'. Some of the series invited listeners' questions which were answered at the microphone, and every encouragement was given to form discussion groups. This technique was further developed in wartime by 'The Anvil', a discussion series between speakers representing the main branches of the churches to argue controversial questions unscripted and extempore. It was perhaps a little one-sided because even chairmen of such experience and wide outlook as F. A. Cockin, Quintin Hogg, and Professor Victor Murray of Hull could not ensure that every point of view was raised and argued. It aroused great interest and some 4,000 questions were submitted during the first series.

Religious talks broadcast during and after the war had a more intimate and personal approach than before 1939, and were publicised with such titles as 'Why I believe in God', 'Christians in a World at War', 'What the Churches can learn from the War', 'Towards a Christian Britain', 'People Matter', and 'The Hope of a New World'. A further change of emphasis was noticeable towards the end of the decade when, in addition to the personal note as in a long series 'My Faith and my Job', the scientific outlook crept in with such titles as 'What is Man?', 'Man Without God', 'Science and the Christian Faith', 'Atomic Warfare', and 'Life after Death'. The more objective philosophic aspects of the problems which concerned thinking people were able to be broadcast in the Third Programme after 1946 with such appropriate titles as 'Christianity as a Basis for Democracy' by Professor Reinhold Niebuhr; 'Liberal Tradition in Theology' by Canon C. E. Raven; 'The Relation of the Christian Religion to the History of Mankind' by Professor Butterfield, and 'The Process of Evolution' by Dr Julian Huxley. Surely the policy on religious talks had undergone remarkable changes since the days when controversy was barred. From 1947, after twenty-five years of broadcasting, expressions of anti-religious opinion were permitted within the context of a discussion or series where both points of view were represented.

Another development in the re-building of organised religion after the war was an item of Christian news and commentary on Sunday afternoons. Dr Nathaniel Micklem of Oxford started the series in 1945, and it was carried on by Professor John Foster of Glasgow. It surveyed the churches at work and reported interesting projects and experiments. Changed to a later hour on a week night, the audience dwindled and the item ceased after two years. It was evident at that time that news of the churches might inform the interested but not instruct the ignorant.

There was still need for some form of presentation that would subdue if not silence the critics, and proclaim the Gospel in such a vivid way that none could fail to recognise its redeeming power. It was in wartime that the opportunity came, and from a person who had made her name and achieved popularity as a writer of detective fiction. Dorothy L. Sayers had submitted a nativity play, *He That Should Come*, which proved a suitable and successful production for Christmas 1938. Two years later, Dr James Welch, then Director of Religious Broadcasting, enquired whether she would think of writing a series of plays on the life of Jesus to be broadcast in the Children's Hour on Sundays. Miss Sayers agreed to prepare the plays, but said that she must introduce the character of Jesus in person, and use modern speech with full dramatic realism. She took great care in the study and handling of the sources, and ably overcame the difficulties involved in writing plays on such a sacred, almost sacrosanct, theme. When the first five were ready for production and the cycle entitled *The Man Born to be King* was due to begin with the story of the Nativity on the Sunday before Christmas 1941, a press conference was held and, though some of the critics who attended were ready to commend the venture, others saw fit to condemn the plays out of hand, without even having read or heard them. They were classed as irreverent, blasphemous, and vulgar, and it was urged that they should be cancelled as unsuitable material for broadcasting. The BBC had to take notice of such protests, however superficial, and indeed so much doubt was cast on the series that a question was asked in Parliament about the advisability of allowing them to be heard. It was too late to cancel the series even if that had been considered necessary, but the second and third plays were hastily sent to members of CRAC for their comments and, when these were found to be favourable, it was decided to proceed with the whole cycle of twelve plays, and the second was broadcast a fortnight after the original scheduled date. At a special meeting of CRAC, the members pledged their full individual and public support to the content and presentation of the plays. Thus the series began with the press opposed to it, but with a group of leading churchmen of different denominations behind it. It is a remarkable and dramatic story in itself how the protests and opposition died down and turned into almost universal approval. The chief criticism at the outset came from those who regarded the impersonation of the voice of Jesus as sheer blasphemy. Many letters were received from individuals and from some denominations, such as the Baptists and the Free Church in Scotland. Huge petitions of protest were organised and delivered to the BBC and to members of Parliament. They contended that not only was it wrong to hear the voice of Jesus portrayed by a human voice, but that the Word of God in the Scriptures was verbally inspired and must on no account be altered. This was the modern equivalent of the old Hebrew idea that the name of God was so sacred that it must never be heard on human lips.

The actor Robert Speaight depicted the voice of Jesus with such devout reverence and deep devotion that the fears of most listeners were soon dispelled. The attitude of those who protested may perhaps have been aggravated by the law which prohibited the representation on the stage in Britain of any Person of the Trinity. It was felt by most people, however, that the mystery plays of the middle ages and the more modern passion play at Oberammergau had largely overcome this difficulty. There was also reverent presentation of religious themes in some notable films. So the production of the play cycle went on, undertaken by the Drama Department of the BBC. Val Gielgud, then Director of Drama, undertook the production and dealt with the scripts as with any other assignment. He acknowledged the singular atmosphere the plays had inspired at rehearsal, and he himself testified to a change in his attitude to the story behind the plays.

The actors who took part were chosen strictly on merit as radio artists, not on their allegiance to the Christian faith. They included many popular microphone personalities of sound radio: Laidman Browne as the Evangelist, Cecil Trouncer as Herod, Valentine Dyall as one of the Wise Men, Lilian Harrison as Mary, and Bryan Powley as Joseph. Robert Speaight, John Laurie, and other well-known names formed the nucleus of a large cast required for the whole cycle. They were added to for particular productions and were supported by what Miss Sayers called 'a wonderful company' who worked like heroes to create the right atmosphere in the short time available for rehearsals under war conditions. All who took part made a valuable contribution to both the artistic and spiritual worth of the series. They were greatly helped by the author, who had supplied elaborate stage directions for every character and scene, showing exactly how she wanted it depicted in the modern idiom. In her introduction to the plays, she dealt comprehensively with the purpose and plan of the cycle, and provided one of the most erudite and enlightened comments that has been written in this century on the theology and dramatis personae of the Gospel story. She asserted that the theology of the New Testament was 'enormously advantageous' so long as it was 'complete theology', and the dramatist set out not to point a moral but to tell a story in the best possible way. She added that the drama must not be subordinated to the theology, but the writer must hope that it will emerge undistorted from the dramatic presentation of the story. Her technique was to keep the ancient setting of the events, and to give the modern equivalent of the contemporary speech and manners. Fortunately the English language, with its wide flexible and double-tongued vocabulary, lent itself to the juxtaposition of the sublime and the commonplace, and pleased all but those who felt that the Authorised Version and no other must be used and quoted.

The play cycle was heard by millions of listeners and the reaction of all but a very small minority was embarrassingly appreciative. Never had a broadcast series received such commendation from thousands of letters and many press reporters. The early critics were confounded; the Gospel story had become real in an unique way, and its teaching was made known with simple clarity to both committed and nominal Christians. As one writer expressed it, 'I have learnt more about my religion in half an hour than I did in all the years of Sunday school.' Another wrote, 'Your plays have thrilled me to the core. The very anguage used shocks us out of the worn conventional erms. I was moved and helped by last Sunday's broadcast nore than ever in my life.' Dr Welch reported to CRAC hat letters had come from people of almost every lenomination, age and occupation, from clergy and :haplains, from members of the forces and workers in ndustry, listeners on the Continent, and from many out-iide the churches. Critical comments continued from the Lord's Day Observance and Protestant Truth societies, but his only added publicity to the series, and the result was a bigger audience than ever before for a religious, and ndeed, for any programme broadcast up to that time, apart from the broadcasts of the Royal Family and the Prime Minister. The play cycle was repeated many times n whole or in part, and the appreciative reaction con-:inued, so that it could be said that the proclamation of :he Gospel as drama was teaching at its best, and combined :he basic aims of imparting the Christian message as preaching, teaching, and evangelism.

Teaching by radio in the postwar years used every means, direct and indirect, to attract listeners. New methods were tried and a return to intensive Bible study was a feature of the programmes after the renewal of the :harter to the BBC in 1952. Television only gradually ntroduced religious items, but a series of dramatic episodes, *Jesus of Nazareth*, almost the equivalent in vision of the play cycle, was presented during Lent in 1955, and attracted many viewers. Tom Fleming played the part of Jesus, and the author and producer was Joy Harrington. Such was the change of attitude in ten years to the voice and person of Jesus being heard and seen that little criticism was received and much appreciation resulted. The Gospel as drama had been discovered after experiment and sometimes failure to be able to teach out of the air.

CHAPTER VIII

RADIO EVANGELISM

Success and Failure of an Experiment

'Except ye be converted'

At a meeting of clergy after the war, a Church of Scotland Minister asked why the BBC did not concentrate its religious effort on personal salvation, and set up a conversion bureau. A similar question had been raised by Dick Sheppard some twenty years earlier when he asserted that 'in broadcasting, Christianity has perhaps the greatest instrument for conversion ever placed in the hands of man in the whole history of Christendom'. He had argued that the task of the church was to get over the message to those still outside its influence, and that the broadcast service could bring the everlasting Gospel right into the homes of the people, and be used in this way. On the other hand, Canon Rowland Grant wrote in *Radio Times* in 1926, 'it is unlikely that the mechanical can ever take the place of the personal, and nothing can ever supersede the presence of the preacher'. This points to the basic difficulty of radio evangelism, and it was probably the reason why little attempt was made to use the microphone deliberately for this purpose until the BBC had been in existence for nearly thirty years.

In the report of the Church of England on the postwar situation, *Towards the Conversion of England*, published in 1945 as 'a plan dedicated to the memory of William Temple', who had encouraged its preparation, reference was made to the need for more than home mission work as such, and a big campaign was recommended to recover the soul of a war-scarred generation. Parochial missions and village evangelism were urged, and emphasis was laid on the importance of 'translating technical theological expressions into terms understood by ordinary people', but it was pointed out that there were obstacles to village evangelism in the lack of leadership, in disunity, and the fact that all parish priests were not equally equipped for this kind of work. The report asserted that a new voice and fresh approach would often supply 'the needed spark to set aflame a carefully laid fire'. In dealing with evangelism among children and youth, it was stressed that Christian home life was the natural and normal introduction of the child into the family of God, and that the church had an unprecedented opportunity of evangelising youth at a time when there was decay in home life, and the influence as to which young people were subjected were becoming increasingly materialistic. Radio was not mentioned in this section of the report, such were the doubts that still existed as to its efficiency, but it was stated in the chapter on broadcasting that 'the true task of religious radio is missionary and evangelistic, especially for those who do not attend church, though broadcasting can only plough the land, and sow the seed, and the church in its parochial aspect must tend and reap'.

The Scottish Church Commission already referred to, 'God's Will in our Time', gave a more theological assessment of the situation. Its report was presented to the General Assembly of that Church in 1942, and asserted that the task of the church was primarily to invite men to place their whole trust in the redeeming love of God,

and that 'the vital place of evangelism and missionary
endeavour in presenting the Gospel to those outside the
church was one of the leading requirements for effective
church life'. It also spoke of the adequate fulfilment of
parochial responsibility, and the full use of opportunitie
for evangelism 'for the sake of the church's influence on
the life of the community and the nation'. A distinction
was drawn between what was termed the 'worshipping
and the 'recruiting' church. The latter required a different
technique, a new form of preaching, and an emphasis on
personal contact and individual conversion. Specially
trained evangelists were needed for such intensive mission
work, and the full co-operation of the laity and organised
groups in the community was necessary for successful
results.

A surprising omission from both reports was the use of
radio for evangelistic purposes. A reference was made in
the Scottish report to the 'multiplying of the means of
communication throughout the world, as producing a
cosmopolitan culture and so creating standards that were
new in most spheres of life', but this was not specifically
applied to evangelism. The English report concluded it
section on radio with the observation, 'Religious Broad
casting has increasingly to learn how to use its own
medium properly.' This was a significant statement so far
as evangelism was concerned. It was true that religious
thought and practice had changed from a simple – and
often rather superficial – proclamation of the Gospel in
the period between the wars to a personal challenge of
the power of Christ to reign in the whole life of the indi
vidual, and attempts had been made to present this
challenge by radio; but something was lacking either in
the medium or in the presentation. Community Hymn
Singing had stirred many who listened; sermon courses
had moved some who heard them so deeply that they had
expressed their intention of living the Christian life; but

there had been no follow-up by the churches. Question and answer, and simple explanation of difficult terms, including the word 'conversion', had been tried and had left an influence on some of the listening audience, but their effect had soon been dissipated. The remarkable response to the play cycle *The Man Born to be King* was the exception. It had presented the Gospel in a new dimension, and had affected many people so deeply that they confessed to what amounted to conversion. It became evident that, before the microphone could be used effectively to bring in the lapsed and the lost, some hard thinking and bold experiment was necessary to determine the target and scope of radio evangelism.

The time was ripe for action. There was no doubt that many who had come through the terrible experience of total war and had survived the devastating power of modern weapons emerged with a deeper and surer faith. This was abundantly clear in the humble thankfulness and profound gratitude which marked the end of hostilities. But when peaceful conditions returned and those who had fought were reunited with their families, it took a long time for new houses to be built and home life to be reestablished. The claims of the church often went unheeded, and the much-longed-for new order tarried. The churches had anticipated a big increase in members but, while older people maintained their loyalty and parents were anxious to send their children to Sunday school, there seemed to be little inclination for churchgoing among the younger 'veterans' of the war and indeed, organised religion as such appeared to have lost its appeal. Here was an opportunity for radio to come to the aid of the churches, and bring the Gospel of Christ's redeeming love to the postwar generation. Broadcasting had been a source of much strength and encouragement in the dangers and isolation of war, but the churches still had doubts about the value of this modern method of communication as a means of evangelism, and no great desire for co-operation had been apparent.

Experiment was the only way to get evidence and it was again in a region that it was carried through. The religious section in Scotland took the initiative with the support of the Scottish Advisory Committee. The organiser, Ronald Falconer, worked in close contact with the Director of Religious Broadcasting in London, Francis House, who had succeeded Dr James Welch in that position. He welcomed the experiment and offered to help in every possible way. How such a project should be tackled had to be decided. Could it be fitted into the existing religious output or must it be organised as a separate venture? For whom was it intended and how should they be made aware that it was meant for them? Audience research had claimed that more than half of those who listened regularly to religious broadcasts were outside the active membership of the churches. How could these people be won for Christ? And after a war of such cruelty and tragedy, how were those who had lost their faith to be helped to recover it? After much thought and study, three broad categories emerged as the target for the experiment, and the aim of the Radio Mission became threefold: 'to challenge the careless, to reclaim the lapsed, and to strengthen the faithful'.

The problem of how to get over the message of salvation to such diverse types of listener was the real crux of the effort. Previous attempts were carefully examined, from the methods of the great evangelists like Wesley and Gipsy Smith to the men who used the hard-hitting eloquent appeal, and the polished technique of postwar evangelists like Billy Graham in America. It was decided to prepare and present some sixty items of widely varied type, but all based on the theme of urgent personal challenge. These would be broadcast by experienced and effective radio preachers as missioners, each with assignments suited to his particular ability and all adding up to an intensive effort to bring listeners to the point of decision.

It was realised that many forms of presentation would be necessary to attract and retain the interest of those for whom the items were intended. It was anticipated that 'the faithful' would be regular listeners because they were professing Christians, though how loyal to their promises was difficult to assess. For them, the traditional type of church service was likely to be most convincing, so the mission must include such broadcasts. For the 'lapsed', a different approach was required. Many of them had expressed a real desire to return to the Christian way of life – possibly after being moved by some preacher or programme – and they usually added in their letters that it was the personality of the speaker which had helped them. So the best radio preaching must find a place in the mission. 'The careless' were the most difficult category to cater for. About the only fact to go on was that they had often overheard religious items while otherwise occupied, possibly having forgotten to switch off their sets. As one such listener wrote after hearing a good speaker, 'I usually switch off whenever I hear the Rev. so-and-so, because I can't bear his moralising, but you caught me filling my pipe. I left the set on until I had finished the operation and, by that time, I had been gripped by his simple sincerity.' This frank expression gave a pointer to one of the essentials to entice people to listen at their own firesides – natural sincerity issuing from the personality of the speaker, challenging the careless in a way they would find difficult to resist. So the search began for the most suitable radio missioners – men with a message, with real sincerity and, above all, a deep personal devotion and complete dedication to the task of winning men for Christ. It was estimated that some 300 clergymen and laymen had been used in religious broadcasts in Scotland over a period of five years, and some thirty would be needed for

the mission. Reports had been kept on their previous performance and these, together with the comments of
listeners and audience reaction, helped in the selection
and the assignments allotted to each so that their special
gifts and talents could be fully used.

The detailed programme of the Mission was worked out
after much thought and prayer. The general title chosen
was 'This is the Way', and its application to the individual,
'Walk Ye In It'. The evening addresses were to deal with
personal belief, and four dramatic presentations were
given with the title 'You Were There'. It had been decided
to integrate the mission items with the current religious
output, and the People's Service, the Sunday Half-hour,
Lift up Your Hearts, and Saturday Evening Prayers were
brought within the scope of the effort, while children and
youth were catered for in their own programmes. It was
known that, when such vital subjects as Immortality
and Forgiveness were included in talks series, hundreds
of letters were received by the speakers from non-
churchgoers, often from people who had been hurt or
crushed by the cruel circumstances of life. Such themes
had therefore to find a place in the mission, and there had
also to be items for the sick and housebound, a loyal
captive audience that could not be neglected. It proved a
complicated task to try to meet every need, and yet always
keep in the forefront those who were the particular target
of the experiment.

Not only were the most detailed and careful preparations required by the BBC, but the churches had to be made
aware of their opportunity, because true and full conversion was still the result of personal encounter, and had
to be prepared for and followed up if it was to be permanent. So the Scottish religious staff and local clergymen
addressed presbyteries and ministers' fraternals, elders
unions, woman's guilds, and other interested groups
and urged that, with the help of press and microphone

publicity, they and their congregations should take full advantage of the mission. Liaison officers appointed by the General Assembly of the church also helped to bring the details of the effort to the attention of both ministers and laity in their areas. If the project was to be successful, the whole membership must be alerted to use the broadcasts as a means of witness in every parish. This was in line with the policy of the BBC to be the handmaid of the churches. Thus all the machinery of press and radio was geared to make the mission widely known over the whole country. Leaflets were prepared and distributed; information was made available for publication in national and local news-papers, in church magazines and periodicals, and regular announcements told listeners the names of those taking part, the scope of the venture, and when and in what programme to expect the broadcasts.

Careful consideration was given to the timing of the mission. The usual period for such special efforts was during Lent leading up to Easter. Autumn was however chosen, perhaps because Lent was not strictly observed in Scotland, but mainly on account of other evangelistic missions being held at that time. There was a 'Glasgow for Christ' parish mission and a 'Christian Commando' campaign in progress in that city and similar projects were taking place in other parts of Scotland. The radio mission would coincide with the climax of these local efforts, and the fact that it would come at the start of the winter's activities in parish and congregation increased the prospect of success if the churches would co-operate to the full. Every denomination except the Roman Catholic was ready to participate and provide speakers, and most of them were represented in the actual broad-casts. Preliminary talks were given during September 1950, and the whole of October was devoted to the mission proper with a follow-up in November and December. Among those who took part were such well-known radio personalities as Ronald Selby Wright, the former Radio Padre; Dr George MacLeod of the Iona Community; Professor James Stewart of Edinburgh; George Duncan of Keswick Convention fame; Tom Allan, a minister deeply involved in the Glasgow campaign, and Dr A. C. Craig of the British Council of Churches and Glasgow University. All were brought together to discuss the mission, give their comments on the detailed programme and, at a final conference retreat, become welded into a conscious team for this important task.

So the mission began. The theme of the Sunday morning services was a positive exposition of the Christian way of life, and the presentation in the evening took the form of discussions between a parson and a layman on their personal beliefs. Other items both on Sunday and week-days supported these main broadcasts by dealing with different aspects of the themes and their practical outcome in daily living. The sermons and talks as well as the praise and dramatic interludes were direct and virile in their appeal, not the hot-gospeller type urging and demanding personal decision, but penetrating and persuasive to attract listeners of every category and those at every stage of religious experience.

The reactions of the public were very mixed. There was much commendation and a certain amount of criticism. After one of the Sunday morning services, over a hundred letters were received and at least six came from people who said they had undergone a form of conversion. They included a former atheist and a member of the Communist party. As was anticipated, church adherents often ex-pressed appreciation of a challenging and convincing sermon, while non-churchmen found the same broadcast dull and uninspiring. Thus many of the faithful were strengthened, but the careless were left unmoved. The evening services, on the other hand, by their unconventional informality, brought adverse comment from church members but a generally favourable reaction from those outside. Several families became active members of local congregations after hearing these discussions, and some whose membership had lapsed were reclaimed and returned into the fellowship. The dramatic items earned approval from both those on the fringe and those indifferent to organised religion, while strong disapproval came from some of the faithful. The net result was that almost every item attracted or repelled, the usual pattern of radio items.

One satisfactory outcome of the mission was that more people than usual had heard the broadcasts. What impact they made is not easy to assess, but few actual conversions were reported. Much useful information was however obtained and valuable lessons were learned. It was found that when congregations were willing to make full use of the mission, remarkable results could follow. The items did indeed become talking points among neighbours and friends and, what was more important, among operatives in factories, workshops, warehouses and offices. They also provided an easy introduction for parish visitation. The sad fact was that so few congregations had agreed to cooperate. Where missioners and liaison officers did persuade them to organise such efforts, many benefits were apparent. To sum up the experiment, it was felt that, while the idea was feasible and practical, many churches which had approved and supported it in theory, had failed to participate in their parish areas. There was also little evidence that the opportunity was taken to work and pray for revival, so that those who were sincerely moved by the broadcasts had no one to turn to in their desire to change their way of life.

The Glasgow churches campaign provided a somewhat different picture. There the congregations using the broadcasts reported much valuable assistance in their effort. Nominal members and others were brought again into the orbit of church life; the faithful were strengthened, and the spiritual pulse quickened. This was evident from the larger attendances at Communion services, and more young people entering classes for catechumens. In the follow-up period, a service of confirmation and admission to church membership was broadcast.

There were some useful long-term results. Another mission was planned and carried through in 1952. It gave its aim as just the reverse of the earlier experiment. It made 'the faithful' the main target, and its method was to fan out from the centre, using loyal church members to find the careless and indifferent on the circumference. As before, the full co-operation of congregations was vital to success. When that was forthcoming, marvellous results in decisions and actual conversions followed, but otherwise there was little lasting effect. The British Council of Churches' report, 'Christianity and Broadcasting', summed up this need: 'Evangelistic purpose cannot fully be achieved without the establishment of a vital relationship to a local church. Radio brings many people within hearing of the Gospel, but if the person who hears cannot make contact with a virile Christian community, a decisive opportunity may be lost, and a barrier created against any future readiness to hear the Good News. The greatest need of religious broadcasting – and an essential one – is a revitalised church'. Perhaps the Scottish experiment was made too soon, or was man's attempt to hasten the revival of religious life, which only the Spirit of God can direct. It was made at a time when radio had to contend with the novelty of television. What did emerge was the 'Tell Scotland' movement, which kept alive the need for direct evangelism. Was the small TV screen an appropriate method of propagating the Gospel? Could the claims of Christ be brought 'literally' home to viewers, the majority of whom were probably not attached to any church? Might a mission on television be organised on the lines of the radio experiments? These and other questions were very much in the minds of those responsible for framing the policy of religious broadcasting in both the BBC and the commercial television companies, and still call for an answer.

CHAPTER IX

UNITY
AND UNIVERSALITY
The Field is the World

'That ye all may be one'

United effort by the churches was a feature of the experiments in radio evangelism, though emphasis on unity had been the declared policy of the BBC since the start of religious broadcasting. In 1923 Archbishop Davidson had been persuaded by the General Manager to convene a committee representing denominations in the main stream of the Christian tradition. The request of the Vicar of St Martin's for broadcast facilities was approved by this mixed body, and the vision of Dick Sheppard resulted in preachers of different communions being invited to share in these services. This was an uncommon demonstration of unity at that period and, as has been noted, was followed by a similar choice of ministers to broadcast from St Cuthbert's, Edinburgh, and later from St Martin's, Birmingham.

Great occasions of joy or sorrow, of crisis and concern, also revealed a remarkable unity between Christians of different traditions. Out of the bitter experience of the First World War had come a desire for closer co-operation and deeper thinking on current problems. This emerged in the COPEC meetings, already referred to, in Birmingham in 1924, attended by some 200 delegates from most of the

Christian denominations. Two years later, a courageous effort was made by the BBC to place the General Strike above party politics and class bitterness by broadcasting a united service of reconciliation. It was at the Coronation of 1937, however, that a vast listening audience became closely knit in deep loyalty, and this was even more apparent in the Coronation of 1953. On that occasion, vision was added to sound, and the ceremony was seen and shared in by people of every denomination or none.

In 1938, Dr J. D. Jones of Bournemouth, a prominent clergyman of the Congregational Church, gave a series of talks on unity. He asserted that there was a definite drawing together of the churches. Sir Francis Younghusband, the distinguished Indian administrator, expressed at a congress of faiths the same views in a wider context when he said, 'The spirit of world fellowship is the only sure foundation of a better world order'. He wanted to bring together urgently men of good-will in every land, but the outbreak of war made that impossible though it soon brought unity of another kind. Because of security restrictions, listeners of every denomination and sect had to hear the one programme available. United services of intercession, days of prayer for deliverance and later humble thanksgivings for victory revealed real unity. People began to realise that the strength and comfort of the faith were of more importance than arguments about ritual and dogma. The practical outcome while the war was still at its height in 1941 was that four of the great Christian traditions – Anglican, Orthodox, Lutheran, and French Protestant – were able to join in a united broadcast service, and later that year the world aspects of unity were illustrated in a service with addresses by an Indian, a Chinese, and a Japanese Christian.

When hostilities ended, it was to be expected that those with strong denominational loyalties should express doubts about the wisdom of these efforts towards closer unity. Elements of disunity again became apparent, and the BBC was once more faced with claims for religious items to be allocated on the basis of numbers and prestige rather than on ability to communicate the Gospel by radio. But the British Council of Churches had been inaugurated in 1942, largely through the initiative and enthusiasm of Archbishop Temple, and the ecumenical movement was well established. Broadcasting could take some of the credit for the setting up of this and other councils to seek Christian solutions to national and world problems. Radio reflected a remarkable amount of united witness and an increasing area of good-will and co-operation was gradually being created. Many series on the urgent need for deeper unity were broadcast. Titles like 'The Churches and Peace', 'Fellowship across Frontiers', 'Christian Reconstruction in Europe', were chosen, and speakers from many countries used the microphone to place unity in its world context. Bishop Shen of Shensi in China made a strong plea for unity in the younger churches as a matter of life or death, and Dr Van Dusen of New York broadcast a series claiming that world Christianity was the only real hope for the future. He urged that not only leaders of the churches but also the laity must show their willingness to work and witness in united effort and action. Services for unity became a regular feature at the great Christian festivals, especially at Whitsuntide, and often included contributions from such widely separated countries as Sweden, Switzerland, and West Africa – all joining in common acts of worship and giving to listeners a great sense of oneness in Christ. By this modern method of communication, the prayer of the Master that 'ye all may be one' was being realised more fully and rapidly than for many centuries.

Universality is the essence of the Christian Gospel. As Dr Scott Lidgett wrote in *The Listener* in 1933, 'The annihilation of space and time as obstacles to human fellowship has made the world one.' In technical terms as in the realms of the spiritual, there are no boundaries to the reception of wireless signals. Empire broadcasting began officially in 1932 just ten years after radio programmes had started. It was the culmination of much experiment and exchanges of messages between distant stations, many of them picked up in this country by keen amateurs on home-made sets. They came from people in far-off places, thrilled to have such a contact with their native land. These men were pioneers of a new empire link and had discovered how the technical resources of radio could be harnessed to serve humanity. Wireless waves travelling at the rate of light into space and bouncing back to earth seemed to have an affinity with the creative spirit of God hovering over the world, able to link in a novel kind of fellowship men of every race and colour, of every tribe and family, whatever their outlook or religion.

The purpose of overseas broadcasting was to project Britain to all who could hear outside this tiny island, and its aim was to transmit the best of our way of life. It was therefore natural that religious items should become a feature of these programmes and their inclusion was welcomed, but raised all the old problems of form and practice as well as many new ones. To whom should these items be directed? To Christians living abroad with home church ties, or to any who might be able to hear them – pagan and Christian, Jew and Gentile, Moslem and Hindu? Were the broadcasts to be aimed at the inhabitants of the Empire, the majority of whom were non-Christian though loyal to one earthly monarch? Would the result be to bring people closer together or to emphasise their differences? Again, if the Christian religion was to be the radio pattern, what form of worship should be used? What should be the content of sermons and talks on religious subjects? It could not be denied that the projection of Britain was not always suitable for emergent nations and primitive peoples. Could the opportunities of this new medium be taken to help the missionary work of the churches? And if this was a major purpose, should the emphasis be on evangelism, or would the broadcasts be merely a reflection of life and worship in a so-called Christian country?

These matters had to be studied and a policy worked out before religion could form a regular part of Empire radio. It was obvious that listeners in territories belonging to Britain must have the first priority because of their loyalty to the Crown. A big technical obstacle had, however, to be overcome before programmes could be heard at convenient times throughout the Empire. The variation in time between east and west made the provision of suitable transmissions a major operation. Much experiment was necessary and many people helped by sending in useful reports on reception conditions and the kind of items they most enjoyed. After many alterations and adjustments, a programme policy was thrashed out.

The first religious service broadcast to the Empire was on New Year's Day 1933, and was conducted by Pat M'Cormick, then at St Martin's. In April of that year, a service in commemoration of Anzac Day beamed for listeners in Australia was relayed from St Clement Dane Church, London, and a Zeebrugge commemoration service from St Mary's Church, Dover, in the same month. No regular pattern emerged, however, until 1935 when St Paul's Cathedral became 'the parish church of the Empire' with a weekly service for overseas listeners. To ensure the widest coverage, this act of worship was recorded and repeated at suitable times. This might seem at variance with the rule that worship to be real must be 'live', broadcast direct from church or studio, and not 'canned', but recordings were necessary if the needs of the world-wide audience were to be met. When the Empire Service began, the Director General of the BBC, Lord Reith, wrote in *The*

Listener, 'If we succeed in dispelling some of the isolation and loneliness which is the lot of our kindred overseas . . . if we can induce among the constituent parts of the Empire a greater understanding and a greater sympathy, then our efforts are amply rewarded'. This aim was fully realised in such items as the Christmas Day link-up and on important national occasions with religious content – coronations, thanksgivings and commemorations. Many letters and messages of appreciation were received after such broadcasts, not only from people who had recently left the homeland, but also from others who had been abroad for many years and were deeply moved by the recollection they gave of things cherished long ago. So the hearts of Britons abroad were stirred by sharing in worship long neglected and now renewed, and they were quite definite in their preference for services from churches rather than those conducted in a studio. In addition to the regular transmissions from St Paul's, churches in many parts of the country became focal points for overseas relays, and the denominations contributed their particular form of worship for every zone of the Empire. No attempt was made to get converts, or even to direct those who listened to seek membership of a church in the country of their adoption, far less in one of their original allegiance. A new fellowship of the Spirit was however being created, working through modern means and bringing the worship of God and the Christian Gospel to the most scattered and diverse community ever known.

If war conditions meant severe limitation of listening at home, communication with our territories abroad was even more drastically curtailed, though there was more need than ever to bind together the separated peoples of the Empire and to rally them behind the war effort. Broadcasting with its power to overstep boundaries was an obvious method to achieve this; a firm faith was also essential in days of loneliness and danger, and religion by radio could supply this. A short Daily Service specially for overseas was broadcast, and the whole Empire shared in special days of prayer for deliverance and victory. Community hymn-singing of popular and well-loved hymns forged a strong emotional link, and the fundamental tenets of the faith expounded in the context of a total war cemented the unity and resolution of our peoples into a mounting determination to win. Final victory brought deep and sincere expressions of thanksgiving from every part of the Empire, and the freedom that followed the liberation of occupied territories was celebrated with profound gratitude to God. There was apparent at this time a fierce desire to maintain the liberty and peace that had been won at so big a price, and it was realised that the kingdom of God was not only able to bring salvation to the individual but also to usher in the reign of justice and truth all over the world. Overseas broadcasts reflected this ideal and purpose, and it was relevant to the postwar struggle of ideologies that talks on our Christian standards and institutions should be transmitted to the countries of Europe under Communist domination. An important series of this kind 'British Church Leaders Speaking', was given world coverage, with Archbishop Temple, Dr Nathaniel Micklem, Dr J. H. Oldham and others taking part. Christmas and Easter services were also relayed to Europe from the Russian Orthodox Church in London, and the orbit of Overseas Broadcasting was extended from the Empire to all the nations of the world. Radio had put a girdle round the earth, not in Puck's forty minutes, but in less than four seconds, to bind together free men of goodwill in the unseen bonds of Christian love.

CHAPTER X

THE WIDER IMPACT

Varying Yields

'Let them grow together until the harvest'

Broadcasting is a scattering abroad over the whole field. It is there for the taking or leaving, and the individual at the receiving end can accept or reject what is heard or seen, can react passively or with appreciation or criticism, whether the speaker is a member of the Royal Family, a Prime Minister or a bishop, a shop steward or a soccer idol. Some of the benefits and defects inherent in radio in general and in religious broadcasting in particular have already been noted. When sceptics and agnostics hear or see items not intended for them, and treat them with contempt or derision instead of turning off their sets, the only consolation is that their hostile reaction is confined to a few people in isolation and is soon forgotten. There is always however the chance of the opposite result – that some of the seed sown on hard, stony ground may yield a harvest. Fears in the early days that the wrong type of people might hear these items were gradually dissipated, and refusal of the Chapter of Westminster Abbey to grant facilities for the broadcast of a royal wedding in 1923 turned in due course into a desire, almost a demand, that such important events should be made available for the largest possible audience.

Coronations are the best example of the wider impact

of radio, with their mixture of pageantry, festivity, holi-
day, and a spirit of sincerity and goodwill based on common loyalty and the deep religious significance of the
crowning. The Coronations of 1937 and 1953 have been
referred to but their presentation deserves closer study.
The Coronation of King George VI was, at that time, the
most intricate assignment which had ever been undertaken
by the BBC. The aim of the planners was to enable everyone of the King's subjects at home and in the remotest
outposts of the Empire to see 'with the inner eye of the
mind', as it was described in the Year Book, the pomp
and solemn ritual of the ceremony at which the Sovereign
dedicated his life to them. Not only the people of Britain
wanted to hear every detail of this great occasion; it had
to be made available for the countries which had sent
members of their royal families and other representatives
to the ceremony. A huge technical control unit was in-
stalled in the Abbey with facilities for some fourteen
countries to hear commentaries in their own language. Six
short-wave transmitters were used for this purpose and
overseas listeners were linked to the home programme so
that literally millions were united in sharing by radio the
events of Coronation Day. More than twenty countries
participated in the transmissions and recorded repeats, so
that they were heard by more people than any other item
in the whole history of broadcasting. Crowds gathered in
such far separated places as Auckland, Nairobi, Bathurst,
Singapore, and Ottawa, and reported an unforgettable
experience cementing the loyalty of the Empire and the
increasing friendship of foreign peoples for Britain.

The real significance for us of this unique occasion in
the life of the nation was its religious element. The elaborate planning and detailed organisation was to emphasise
the Christian basis of the crowning. The procession to the
Abbey made colourful listening, but it was in the sacred
precincts of that ancient shrine that the new monarch

was hallowed, crowned, and presented to his people. The commentary of Dr Iremonger was spoken with such choice language and deep reverence that the action of the service, the superb praise and the singing of the choirs, and the actual crowning by Archbishop Lang were made very real and fully understood. They conveyed a sense of wonder and solemnity that hushed the listening millions to silent appreciation. The varied rites of the ceremony each contributed to the sacred and sacramental nature of it all – the anointing, the giving of the sword, the investing of the royal robe, the orb and the cross, the ring, sceptres, and the emblems of justice and mercy, and finally the Bible – all had symbolic meaning and made the whole an act of supreme importance in a Christian country.

Television was still in its early stages in 1937, and it was possible only for cameras to be placed at Hyde Park Corner to take shots of the Royal Procession as it returned to the Palace. By 1953, sight had been fully added to sound and, in addition to all the microphones, there were some twenty cameras inside and outside the Abbey, so that the marvellous pageantry, the brilliance of the crowning, and the religious rites, hitherto reserved for the few who could be present, were seen by millions of viewers as well as heard by countless listeners all over the world. Nearby countries such as France, Holland, and West Germany saw the ceremony with the help of a cross-channel link, and a telefilm was made and flown out to Canada and the United States for viewing there the same evening. Inside the Abbey, Richard Dimbleby guided viewers through the service, but the unique glory of the occasion was the ability of people everywhere, alone or in groups, to share in the action as it proceeded, headed by Archbishop Fisher and other dignitaries of Church and State. It marked as never before the consecration of a whole nation and Commonwealth, and their devotion to a charming young Queen, whose prayer on the eve of her dedication – 'I pray that God will help me to discharge worthily this heavy task that has been laid upon me' – stirred many hearts to a deeper faith and truer loyalty.

The 1953 Coronation had another feature which indicated a closer unity in the churches. While every large denomination except the Roman Catholic was represented in the Abbey, the Moderator of the General Assembly of the Church of Scotland, Professor Pitt-Watson, was allocated the duty of presenting the Bible to her Majesty, thus emphasising the ecumenical nature of the crowning and bringing another national church, which laid great stress on the scriptures and their teaching, into the ceremony. He was not, however, invited to partake of Communion with others participating in the ceremony, a sad reflection on the climate of unity at that time.

Other public events in varying degree brought the Christian religion to the notice of people everywhere and when they were broadcast they attracted much more attention, especially in times of stress and emotion. National days of prayer in wartime and Armistice and Remembrance commemorations impressed even those who had little use for religion. The launching of great ships with the blessing of God upon their voyaging, the opening and dedication of fine buildings, even the singing of hymns at the start of football matches – all helped to give religion its place in the common life of the people. Reports of church assemblies, councils, and conferences, intended primarily for interested church members, could also be heard and seen by the vast overspill of radio and television, and would perhaps influence some who might be listening or viewing.

The underlying assumption was that Britain was a Christian country in spite of T. S. Eliot's assertion to the contrary. Broadcasting began with this assumption in 1922 and, apart from a small vocal number of critics, it was accepted without question by the majority. There is ample

evidence of this from letters to the BBC and audience research reports. Listeners who took the trouble to write
about items that pleased or annoyed them must add up to
many thousands over the years. It is interesting to find
that on personal or religious problems arising from broadcasts, people preferred to write to someone unknown to
them except by voice or vision rather than to their minister
or parish priest. Dr Selby Wright, the Radio Padre, reported
that when he spoke on 'The Hope of Immortality', he had
nearly 1,000 letters of enquiry. After taking the People's
Service, he often had hundreds of expressions of thanks
and sincere longing. An analysis of such correspondence
would reveal a serious groping after a faith to live by and
an anxious search for forgiveness and freedom from the
burden of sin.

Audience research proved a useful method of checking
reaction to programmes. Day-to-day interviews gave a
quantitative return of those listening or viewing and, while
there was a margin of error in the limited sample possible,
they usually confirmed the feelings expressed in letters to
the BBC and by the critics in the press. From the questions
asked about particular items, much information was received about their popularity or otherwise, and about the
trends and habits of those who heard or saw them. In 1943,
it was estimated that about fifty per cent of the whole adult
audience listened to one or more of the services and other
religious items, and that the Sunday Half-hour and Forces
Service were by far the most popular. Special surveys were
also made in 1948 and 1954 into the composition of the
audience for such items. It was found that the overall
majority, especially listeners to these popular items, were
unattached to any church. This indicated the wider impact
of radio in reaching so many outside organised religion.
The most convincing example was of course *The Man
Born to be King* which, as we have seen, was unrivalled in
both its attraction and appreciation. The only general

conclusion that can be drawn from all the evidence is that, however ephemeral and superficial the effect of hearing and seeing religious broadcasts may seem, there has been created in this generation a multitude of men and women who accept what the church stands for, though many of them lack the courage to declare openly their faith, or have been prevented from its active membership by prejudice or some bitter experience. There is little doubt also that the work of the churches has been greatly helped by the climate of acceptance of the standards of Christian life and conduct, if not by positive practice, which the cumulative effect of broadcasting has made possible. It would be reasonable therefore to conclude that listening and viewing by church members has increased their loyalty and strengthened their faith.

The field of broadcasting is the world, and the impact of religion by radio in countries outside Britain deserves some mention because of its influence at home. The Overseas Service of the BBC beamed its programmes to be heard by peoples of every race and religion. Their reaction was conditioned by language, education, and by Christian adherence. Emergent nations had become the missionary objective of many religious bodies, and those subjected to this almost aggressive enterprise over the years were inclined to resist persuasion unless accompanied by benefits such as healing and education. In all the circumstances, the impact of religious broadcasts on backward races in the Commonwealth must have been very slight, and even this was further reduced by the effect of two world wars fought between so-called Christian countries.

Radio was well established in most European nations before 1939. When hostilities began, broadcasting was taken over for propaganda purposes in dictatorship countries. Hitler used the microphone to strike terror into the German people and to bend their wills to make the State their God. Any expression of religious belief was forbidden, though before that time radio had reflected the prevailing climate of loyalty to the Church in Germany. When the occupied countries were freed after the war, a resurgence of Christianity was evident and assisted in the reconstruction of national life. Churches with a common liturgical language like the Roman Catholic had an advantage. The Vatican radio station had both local and wide international coverage, and nations such as Italy, Belgium, and Switzerland, with strong national churches and state-controlled or public service systems of broadcasting, proclaimed regularly the basis and practice of their faith. There was, however, competition from 'pirate' stations, such as Fécamp and Luxembourg, which regarded Sunday as their most important day, and broadcast commercial programmes at times when, in Britain and elsewhere, there was no secular alternative to religious items. Radio Luxembourg included also sponsored programmes supplied by six American sects, among them the Seventh Day Adventists, and the Lutheran Laymen. These were mostly recorded in the United States, were transmitted in various European languages, and without doubt had considerable impact because of their popular presentation.

Another international religious agency, also originating in America and known as 'The Voice of the Andes', could be heard in many countries in Europe and was broadcast on short-wave bands in many languages. Incorporated in 1931 in Connecticut as the World Missionary Fellowship, its programmes were radiated from Quito in Ecuador. Fundamentalist in theology, its aim was personal evangelism through Bible study, the formation of radio groups, and the conducting of correspondence courses. After twenty-five years, the organisers were able to report many world-wide contacts and changed lives, and were then beginning to employ television in co-operation with sponsors in America. The impact of this station by sound radio must have been felt in many countries, and was sustained by *The Missionary Log*, a monthly bulletin distributed through its radio groups. Its programmes were specially directed to those beyond the regular care of the churches – seamen on their voyages, isolated missionaries, garrisons, and radio amateurs, the 'hams' of every country, whose technical enthusiasm could lead to new experiences and religious influence.

A complete contrast to the general pattern of European broadcasting was to be found in the commercial radio of the United States. Time on the air had to be bought, and only those who could afford it and build up programme support were able to attract large audiences and make any impact. Should religion enter this commercial field ? Should Christ be exploited like cars and cosmetics ? Billy Graham gave his reply in characteristic fashion : 'I am selling the greatest product in the world; why shouldn't it be promoted as well as soap ? Why should not the church employ some of these methods that are used by big business or labour unions to promote their products or causes, in order to win men for Christ ?' He used both sound radio and television for evangelism, and his 'Hour of Decision' on Sunday evenings was a feature of one of the coast-to-coast commercial networks for a considerable time.

Some sponsors were willing to include religious items of the popular kind in their programme schedules on the argument that, as the great films like *Ben Hur* and *The King of Kings* had brought good box-office returns, so the dramatic stories of the Bible and novel presentation of the Christian faith by real radio personalities would benefit everyone. But the problem still remained for the churches whether to use commercial sponsorship for religion in competition with other peak-period items. It resolved itself by the emergence of a few outstanding people – men like Henry Emerson Fosdick, Bishop Fulton J. Sheen, Father Coughlin, and Billy Graham. Their success was the result of dynamic, intelligent, dedicated personality with voice and features ideally suited to this new medium of communication. So great was their power to attract huge audiences that sponsors vied to secure their inclusion. Here was an opportunity of proclaiming the Gospel to listeners and viewers 'with whom the churches had few other effective means of contact'. The impact made might be influenced by the very secular programmes in which they were placed, but there is little doubt that they aroused greater interest in religion as such and support for the beliefs they so persuasively presented. It was of course a free-for-all, and the richer churches and sects were able to use the medium to the full with the help of every gimmick and novel technique to get over their message. There was inevitably wide variation in the methods employed. The Presbyterian Church concentrated on preaching and Bible study, while the Jewish Theological Seminary gave their interpretation of Jewish ritual, ceremonial and folklore. The Christian Scientists had no restrictions placed on them as in Britain, and the Lutheran Church was able to present many evangelical series. A typical Sunday in 1952 included in its schedules such varied items as a Presbyterian church service; 'Youth on the March' with choir, Glee Club and sermon; 'Faith for Today' with interviews and Gospel singers; a Lutheran dramatic series, 'This is the Life'; Television Religious Hour; *The Greatest Story Ever Told* – a Biblical drama sponsored by the Goodyear Tyre Co. – and, Billy Graham's Hour of Decision – a motley assortment. An interesting development was the allocation of free time for religion by the commercial companies. The Federal Communications Commission, the licensing authority, regarded 'a little religion as a good thing for everybody', and items of ethical value and religious content qualified for inclusion without payment. This helped many of the poorer sects, but increased the variations of belief and practice offered to the public in that great continent.

By any standards, the impact of this total American

religious output must have been very considerable over the years. Its effect on moral and spiritual life can never be fully assessed, but a marked return to worship emerged in many States after the war, with crowded churches, Sunday schools, instruction classes thronged with students, and congregational life vital and active. In contrast, the large areas of Canada which could hear and view the same programmes do not appear to have experienced this re-vitalising result, so that radio and television may be only one of the causes of this revival of religious life in the United States. The latest indications are that it is a temporary more than a permanent expression of man's need of the power of God to enable him to withstand the pressures and uncertainties of this atomic age, with the mysterious universe becoming a neighbourhood almost overnight.

The summing up of these facts forces us to the conclusion that the scattering abroad of religion by broadcasting has made a considerable impact on this generation. Whatever the ultimate result, it is heartening to realise that the churches and sects in almost every country with a long-established radio service have made a valuable contribution to the standards and poise of modern life, and have given hope and courage to those who have been able and willing to accept religion in this way. The words of Alfred Noyes, penned in the early twenties, are peculiarly applicable: 'To those who have any mental or spiritual vision, broadcasting is the most startlingly vivid scientific indication of the belief that this universe is essentially miraculous, essentially a unity, and responsible in the last analysis only to the supreme miracle of the Single Reality in which we live.'

CHAPTER XI

SOME ELEMENT OF COMPETITION

Vision Splendid

'What do ye more than others?'

The charter granted to the BBC in 1952 as a result of the Beveridge Report indicated that 'provision should be made to permit some element of competition'. This suggestion was the outcome of much political pressure, and was said to have been reluctantly approved by the Prime Minister, Sir Winston Churchill. Its inclusion altered the whole course and character of broadcasting in Britain. Some safeguards were inserted in the final draft of the bill to prevent cut-throat competition, which was contrary to the established practice of radio and television in this country. It applied only to television and was intended to be organised in such a way that advertisers had no power to select the items adjacent to which their advertisements might appear - very different from the American method.

It was generally agreed that religious items must be entirely free from any advertising matter and, both in London and in the regions, high executives declared that it would be quite wrong even to compete in broadcasts about the Christian faith, but the commercial companies modified this good intention by saying that they had to attract an audience on Sundays as well as on other evenings, and they would have to use the 'closed period' from six-fifteen to seven-thirty on Sundays, when advertisements were barred, to build up that audience. So began almost unavoidable competition in religious as in other items, though with advice given by CRAC to both BBC and ITA on the type of programme recommended as most suitable to fill that period.

In spite of the working difficulties described by Canon Roy M'Kay in his book *Take Care of the Sense*, the items became in due course more complementary than competitive, and showed the remarkable diversity possible in the presentation of our faith. The ITV programmes 'About Religion' and 'Sunday Break', brought together a wide and varied cross-section of young people of very different views and background to take part in music, dancing and discussion, usually with a clergyman as leader. This item had at one time the highest viewer rating of any religious programme produced by either BBC or ITV. It was obvious that the companies were willing to experiment more than the BBC, which had transferred many of its well-tried 'sound' religious items to television and was thus able to provide material of greater interest to serious-minded people. So an element of competition continued on different levels and, contrary to expectation, attracted a bigger and wider audience of viewers.

In every other sphere of broadcast production and presentation, competition became more intense. Artists who had been regularly contracted to the BBC were persuaded to accept work with the companies – except for a few exceptional people like Gilbert Harding, who were given exclusive contracts. The interchange soon became general, and popular performers were almost auctioned to the highest bidder and made more money than was ever possible in public service broadcasting. Others did not fare so well. The American pattern was being repeated in Britain, with the stars becoming rich and famous over night, while the rest often found it hard to make end meet. A number of producers and executives left the BBC, and familiar names came on to the screens of the companies as directors and producers. The long experience of the Corporation was being used indirectly to sell goods and make profits.

The first decade of television with some element of competition saw a great change in standards, especially in the BBC which had to alter its policy and methods to show that it could retain its audience against all the resources of commercialism. Audience research and the Tam ratings reported viewing trends, with the novelty of 'advertising spots' and productions by former BBC staff and artistes drawing away audiences from their former loyalties, and the ratio of ITA viewers to those still viewing BBC programmes greater. The Television Act of 1964 following the report of the Pilkington Committee required the ITA to ensure good standards, but the Corporation had the discretion to continue its policy of delegating to producers responsibility for the quality of its programmes. The result was that, in the second decade of competitive television, the older organisation, while retaining many items of very high standard, became more extreme in experiment, especially in drama and the so-called 'kitchen sink' type of programme. It seemed as if there was a deliberate desire to shock, in both language and presentation, on the plea that real life was being depicted, rather than the veneer of Victorian attitudes to youth and sex, to working life and sport. Producers now appeared to include anything that would startle, disturb, and embarrass. The eternal lounge bar, couples in bed, family rows, swearing, squabbling, fighting, and even shooting – not only on Westerns – became commonplace. This was perhaps intended as an imitation of the *avant garde* attitude in America and Europe, but certainly not the kind of programme material acceptable to the average family in this country.

The churches were perturbed at the apparent deterioration in moral and social standards and made strong protests to the BBC. These were reinforced by the energetic action of Mrs Mary Whitehouse, a teacher in a large secondary modern school in Shropshire, who organised a Clean-up TV Campaign, and gave up her post to devote her whole time to this task. She issued a manifesto from the women of Britain calling upon the Postmaster-General to set up a viewers council. She was supported by church people of almost every denomination.

The BBC reacted as was to be expected of a public service corporation accustomed to receiving many letters and telephone messages from the more sensitive members of its massive audience. At the start of the controversy with Mrs Whitehouse, the criticisms were acknowledged and noted, but little was promised. Any large organisation instinctively dislikes those who seem to know better than the experienced staff it employs. The Corporation had been given the responsibility of running its own programmes and was prepared to do this under its charter. Audience research and the weight of opinion in listeners' and viewers' letters and messages did not, so far as can be judged, confirm that the strictures of the National Viewers and Listeners Association were representative of the general reaction of the public.

Mrs Whitehouse's persistence, however, caused some embarrassment to the BBC, and some relief was felt when other movements sprang up as an antidote to her campaign. One began in the new town of Harlow called 'Freedom for Television', and became known as COSMO after the name of the street where its first meeting was held. Another group was formed calling itself TRACK – 'The Television and Radio Committee' – and had behind it Professor Richard Hoggart of Birmingham. These bodies with varying emphasis wanted the BBC to continue to be fully responsible for the standards of its programmes. The controversy then developed into a struggle between opposing factions and the Corporation was able to watch its progress with interest and some concern. There was a good deal of mud-slinging. The Chairman of the Board of Governors, the Director General, the Director of Television, and the Head of Religious Broadcasting were all pilloried – almost every statement they made being used, often out of context, to help the campaign. The late Lord Normanbrook, in his considered statements, tried to make people realise the perennial dilemma of the BBC in having to provide entertainment for its huge audience on both sound and vision with almost infinite variety of tastes and interests. The theatres, cabarets, and night clubs of London are the chief sources of supply for the material required to fill the insatiable schedules of the programme planners. Writers, directors, and producers have to be largely recruited from the West End of the metropolis, and they bring with them the standards currently prevailing there. As a result, the programme offerings are bound to reflect the kind of entertainment provided for London's West End public, though it is often very different in presentation to that found outside London. Broadcasting has, however, to cover the whole country and much of this material proved unsuitable for listeners and viewers in other parts of Britain. To meet the needs of all categories of the audience, every effort was made to place items of sectional interest in the late evening, and warnings were given by announcers of the type of item to be expected. People could of course turn off their sets, but that did not prevent the curious and the careless from continuing to listen or view and complain afterwards. Some also argued that, having paid their licence, they should not have to curtail their home entertainment because of items unsuitable for family viewing.

The dilemma was intensified by various factors. The phenomenal progress in science and technology resulting in automation in many processes made work more monotonous and leisure with congenial activities more essential. The invasion of space had also affected religious, moral, and social values. A reappraisal of this newly discovered dimension was necessary to allay doubts and fears. The prosperity of the postwar years had resulted in the children of servicemen, lacking parental control during the war, now grown up with money to spend, demanding freedom to spend it as they thought best. Born into an age of radio and television, could these young people, many of them of splendid calibre, be retained as listeners and viewers if their interests were not satisfied with 'pop' music available all day on their transistor sets, and the items they wanted on television such as 'Juke Box Jury' and 'Top of the Pops'? And would the pleasure-loving adults be content without the kind of entertainment provided for them in gaming and night clubs, and cinemas and theatres which avoided censorship by assuming club status? The BBC did a great deal to help these newly prosperous people. Music of the Rock and Roll and Beat groups was provided and much pop music on the Light programme, but it was not sufficient for those who tuned in to the pirate stations for continuous records of this kind. Ridicule, satire of the modern type, and parodies of people and occasions, both secular and sacred, were included in such late evening items as 'That was the Week that Was' and 'Not so Much a Programme' and, while they no doubt delighted the artistic and intellectual types of viewer, they were strongly disliked by many others for their unscrupulous language and clever innuendo. Much of this material was concentrated at the weekends, so that on Sundays every type of item was to be found. The protests and fears of thirty years earlier that a continental Sunday would come in Britain had been proved fully justified so far as radio and television were concerned.

As already noted, the commercial companies were under the editorial control of the ITA for programme standards.

but the BBC maintained its practice of retrospective review after items had been broadcast. This seemed to permit the prominence of violence, vulgarity, and viciousness to satisfy a minority section of the viewing public. The Corporation had radically changed its policy in other ways. The prevalent criticism in the twenties was that the Director General gave listeners what he thought they should hear by radio, consistent with artistic merit and the desire to raise public taste in every form of entertainment. His interpretation of the Crawford Committee's recommendation that the BBC should act as 'trustee for the national interest' was to broadcast only the best and to lead public opinion in standards of decency and quality of everything suitable for radio. In the sixties, the criterion seemed to be to follow rather than lead, reflecting trends and opinions proclaimed by the most vocal section of the public. The result was a much wider spread of programme standards and expressions of social conduct and moral values, tolerated by many people in a country where religion and church-going were at a discount compared with thirty years ago. To the churches and Mrs Whitehouse, there seemed to be a lack of leadership, and all the items of undoubted quality and good taste both on sound and television could not compensate for those they criticised. At bottom, the deterioration in standards was the inevitable outcome of that 'element of competition' permitted by the charter of 1952 and the struggle for audience figures it imposed on the BBC.

Much experiment and expansion continued in religious output in spite of the general trend to depreciate religion. The attempts by church groups to link up with the modern outlook of youth by providing new settings to old hymns and broadcasting them with guitar accompaniment were persuasive and helpful. Young listeners and viewers were also given plenty to argue about by adopting the practice of youth fellowships to discuss every subject of moral and social interest, often debunking the Bible and traditional beliefs. Truly the tables had been turned from the days when religious controversy was not permitted.

The World Association for Christian Broadcasting was set up in 1963 to co-ordinate and encourage the fullest use of radio and television 'to proclaim the Christian Gospel in its relevance to the whole of life'. Its aim was world-wide, and it emphasised the need for broad planning, training, study, and research. The increasing challenge of secular standards was being met by an active and forward-looking religious policy so that the future might rise above the problems of the present. A motto of the BBC was still *Quaecumquae*, the apostolic injunction for good individual and social life. Its origin and ideals may have been forgotten in the effort to counter cut-throat competition. In its modern translation, it can serve as a reminder to executives and producers of the ultimate standards necessary to maintain the high reputation of British broadcasting – 'things that are true and noble, just and pure, all that is lovable and gracious, whatever is excellent and admirable, fill your thoughts with these things'. In his book *Broadcast over Britain*, published in 1924, Lord Reith saw the vision of what could be when he wrote, 'There is no telling when the lamps are lit before the Lord, and the message and the music of eternity move through the infinities of the ether, filling the whole earth with the glory of them, as once there appeared a glory in the cloud and a spirit moving upon the face of the waters.'

EPILOGUE

In a foreword to this book, Lord Reith described in his characteristic way how he selected a Director of Broadcasting for Scotland. As the person involved, I may perhaps be allowed to add an epilogue to recount the effects of his choice on a reluctant clergyman to quit the active ministry and leave his parish. If it had not been that I had been invited to Savoy Hill in London in 1925 to discuss with him the possibility of my taking over the post of Director and refused it because I was then waiting to receive a call to a parish, I should again have refused in 1933, but here was another 'call' to national as opposed to parochial service, and I had to accept. He has referred to the interview in Broadcasting House; I also have a humbling and challenging memory of it when he said quite candidly that he did not expect to find a person anything like one hundred per cent of what he wanted, and had to be content with seventy or eighty per cent.

I left Aberdeen and my parish with great regret; I had been very happy there and had made many friends. By way of consolation, he said he would allow me to accept invitations to preach on special occasions, and he told me that I would be directly responsible to him for religious programmes as well as the whole output of the BBC in Scotland. This enabled me to continue my work as a clergyman and, at the same time, use my army administrative experience for the benefit of my fellow men in a very new sphere.

The appointment was criticised both within and outside the church. Why should a minister of religion be taken for a mainly secular post when there were so many vacant parishes? And what was Lord Reith thinking about when he chose a parson to look after radio entertainment? What could he know about the needs of the listening public? I found service under him hard but stimulating. He could make his displeasure felt in no uncertain terms when he was unhappy about the content and standards of the programmes, but he was always ready to commend and encourage good work and initiative, and I looked on him not as a tyrant or dictator but as a fair and just leader, though he was not the kind of man who would suffer fools gladly. He took a deep interest in his staff and knew most of them personally with a specially warm heart for Scots.

The BBC was one of the first public service corporations to function in Britain. It was independent of Government control in its day-to-day operations but ultimately responsible to Parliament which had to vote the licence money required for its maintenance and management. It was inevitable that the regions should be under a large measure of control from London, and had to provide the best programmes available on the meagre allowance (£500 a week for Scotland in the early thirties) or take items from the national networks. The Regional Directors met in London every month to discuss policy. The Director General expected to see me on those occasions and hear how things were going in Scotland, especially on religious matters. He never lost his interest in his native land – which did not lose in consequence – in fact, many of the experiments tried out north of the Border were the result of his encouragement. He had left the Corporation before the war and missed the cramping frustrations of these bitter years. Scotland with his agreement became more than just a region of Britain, and was able to express its distinctive nationality. Its language and customs were given full scope and its traditions in Church and State were increasingly reflected in the broadcast output.

Lord Reith in his foreword criticises the church for not appreciating the recognition of its activities afforded by radio, but the acceptance of anything new is often in inverse ratio to the age and influence of the organisation.

well remember a very troublesome interview with the Scottish Football Association in the thirties to get permission to relay even thirty minutes of an unnamed soccer match each Saturday. Was it surprising that the churches would be wary of permitting outside broadcasts at the will of the BBC? If it had not been for the wisdom and forward looking outlook of some of the great radio personalities of the Church of Scotland, such as Principal John Baillie, Professor Archibald Main, Dr George MacLeod, and Dr Selby Wright, the appeal of religious broadcasting would have been much less and slower to develop. I was privileged to take a major part in guiding the churches to accept this new medium of communicating the Gospel and exploiting every method that could make its message more effective. Whether Lord Reith's choice was justified must be left to the test of time; I can only acknowledge with humble gratitude the opportunity given me to work in such a novel and fascinating service.

Index

INDEX